Recipes from
SAN FRANCISCO'S
GREAT
CHINESE
RESTAURANTS

by the same author

SAUCEPANS AND THE SINGLE GIRL
(with Judy Perry)

THE HOW TO KEEP HIM (AFTER YOU'VE CAUGHT HIM)
COOKBOOK
(with Judy Perry)

Recipes from SAN FRANCISCO'S GREAT CHINESE RESTAURANTS

JINX MORGAN

E.P. DUTTON & CO., INC. / NEW YORK

Library of Congress Cataloging in Publication Data

Morgan, Jinx.
Recipes from San Francisco's great Chinese
restaurants.

1. Cookery, Chinese. 2. San Francisco—Restaurants
—Directories. I. Title.
TX724.5.C5M65 1976   641.5'951   76-9864

ISBN: 0-8415-0441-5

Published simultaneously in Canada
by Clarke, Irwin & Company Limited, Toronto and Vancouver

For Jeff,
whose love, faith
(and chopsticks)
never faltered

Contents

Recipes

Recipes marked (*) are HOT so season to taste

ix

Acknowledgements

Although it's always nice to complete a book and see its finished pages sitting neatly on your desk, the end of this one brings with it a pang of regret. No longer can I visit my friends in Chinatown and justify the treat by saying I'm working.

Without all the charming and generous people I met along the way there would have been no book and, far worse, none of the experiences I treasure. A list of the people who helped would run as long as the book itself, but special thanks go to Douglas Johnson, who shared with me his list of Asian restaurants compiled for the 1970 convention of Asian Scholars at Stanford University; H. K. Wong of the Empress of China; Shirley Lewis Harris, who was always helpful; Chi Wei Wang; George Chan; Jack Chow; Philip Liang; John Tu; Colonel George Chow; Henry and Diana Chung; Joe Jung; Guy Wong; Madame Cecelia Chiang; Al Chan; Ricky Tsuei; Joseph Chou; Edsel Ford Fung; David Lee; Shao Cheng Chang; Leonard and Wy Lum Wong; and Bill Chan.

Cathy Dittemore and Susan Smith helped guide this work through its awkward adolescence and, as always, Carl Brandt was both agent and friend.

Many stalwart chums saw me through both successes and failures, always with good spirits, but among those who were faithful to the end were Fran, Frieda, and Virginia, food-lovers all and jolly good companions.

JINX MORGAN

Oakland, California
March 1976

Introduction

San Francisco's Chinatown bewitched me from the first time I set eyes on it. I was quite small then, only about six or seven years old, and very proud of the new pair of patent leather Mary Janes I was sporting. For some time afterward I felt that they must be enchanted shoes like Dorothy's, for Grant Avenue was as wondrous to me as the Land of Oz.

The street was a carnival of color and movement. Fierce dragons wound around the lampposts and picture-book buildings glowing with blue and red paint were topped with strange, curly roofs. In one shop I stood on tiptoe to view the display of jade trinkets, rice bowls, pencil boxes with mysterious hidden compartments, and funny little open boxes with rows of beads my mother said were used by the Chinese to do arithmetic. Eventually I was disengaged from this tempting emporium, bribed by a pair of flashing red chopsticks. We walked on past the bakery on the corner of Grant and Pacific, where my nose began quivering. Glossy buns and sweet cakes beckoned me to come in and sample them, but I was whisked along by my mother and aunt, who had bigger and better things in mind—lunch.

I don't remember the name of the restaurant and I'm not even sure it still exists, but I do recall the meal we had there. Everything was excitingly different from what we ate at home, and our waiter became my lifelong friend by teaching me how to use my new chopsticks. I drank tea out of a tiny cup, and at the end of the meal opened a magic cookie with a slip of paper inside that read, "Romance would be risky tonight." I've been devoted to Chinese food ever since.

Today San Francisco's Chinese restaurants are no longer con-
fined to the two-dozen-square-block area known as Chinatown.
Chinese restaurants dot every neighborhood, and their cuisine has
expanded far beyond the Cantonese food I ate as a child.

The original settlers of San Francisco's Chinese community
arrived from Canton in the early 1850s, lured by California's gold
rush. They called San Francisco *gum shan,* or the golden hills, but
the promise turned to ashes for the immigrants from the banks of
the Pearl River. As the Chinese made their way to the mining
camps, they were met by a wall of prejudice that would plague
them for generations.

With their dreams of riches defeated, excluded from all but the
most menial jobs, the Chinese resorted to one of the few skills they
were allowed to practice—cooking. The first restaurants were
modest affairs, since most of the immigrants were poor peasants
whose knowledge of Chinese cuisine was limited at best. Some
dishes emerged from this period that would never be recognized in
China. *Chop suey,* which means "miscellaneous fragments," is a
purely American invention, although based on similar Chinese
mixtures. As American tastes for this unfamiliar food developed,
the restaurants became more refined, and elegant establishments
found success alongside their modest neighbors.

Although some people never get any closer to Cantonese cooking than smudged cartons of lukewarm spareribs, *chow mein,* and
fried prawns, authentic Cantonese dishes have great distinction.
Cooks from this area excel in the delicate art of stir-frying and
their seasonings are restrained, allowing the inherent flavors of the
fresh ingredients to come through. Because they were near the sea,
Cantonese cooks were constantly subjected to foreign influences,
and non-Chinese foods such as tomatoes and corn eventually were
assimilated into their menus.

An accident of history further colored the development of Cantonese cooking. In the seventeenth century the Ming dynasty was
overthrown; many government officials were forced to flee their
homes in Peking and seek refuge in Kwantung province, and
especially in its capital city, Canton. Being gentlemen of substance,
they brought their chefs with them. The journey was often a long
one and the chefs, already skilled in Peking's classical style of

cooking, picked up dishes from other regions during their travels. Their influence helped make Cantonese cooking truly cosmopolitan.

In recent years San Francisco's Chinese restaurants have expanded beyond their early preoccupation with Cantonese food and now offer a splendid variety from all parts of China. Newcomers arriving from other regions have brought with them the flavors of their homelands. China is an enormous country, with a diversity of resources and climates. It's only natural that the cuisine of this vast land would be as varied as its people and landscape.

In addition to the Cantonese, or southern, style of cooking, the Chinese divide their country into three other regional cuisines: northern, including Peking, Shantung, and Honan; coastal, which refers to Fukien and Shanghai; and inland, the area around Szechwan and Yunnan. The unique dishes of these areas are now reaching San Francisco (and other American cities) as more and more restaurants sprout, offering authentic menus from these provinces.

In the north an elegant, refined cuisine developed around the court and government life in Peking. The concentration of wealth in the capital allowed chefs there to indulge their most fantastic whims at sumptous banquets. Not content with ingredients they found in their own backyard, they imported provisions from all corners of the country. They justified this extravagance by creating a classical cuisine that became known as Mandarin cooking—the distillation of what was best from every area.

The dishes they developed were light, often cooked with wine, and typically seasoned with garlic, scallions, and chives. Such delicacies as Peking Duck, Spring Rolls, and Chicken Velvet are examples of the northern Mandarin style.

Not everyone in the north was wealthy, however, and for many, rice was a luxury. Wheat was the staple of their diet; noodles, pancakes, and steamed breads and dumplings replaced the grain that was the most important food in the south.

Rice begins to assume its vital role near Shanghai, in the coastal area where the climate favors its cultivation. No meal in the major portion of China is considered complete without a bowl of rice.

It's as much a part of the Chinese culture as bread is to the French. The reason Westerners complain of being hungry an hour after a Chinese meal is that they tuck into their shrimp or duck or pork and ignore the bowl of rice that accompanies it. No Chinese would ever treat this precious grain so cavalierly. They respect it as the staff of life and know that it fills up empty nooks and crannies, insuring a comfortable, well-padded feeling until the next meal comes along.

Fish and shellfish are also important to the Shanghai area that borders the abundant sea. The fish are sometimes roasted, then fried until the bones are crisp enough to be eaten. In Fukien, south of Shanghai, oysters and clams join the parade of seafood; this province on the Formosa Strait is also noted for its light, clear soups.

To the west is the last, but by no means the least, of the four regions—Szechwan. Its four-alarm fare, pungent with hot peppers and vinegar, has its own volcanic appeal. Szechwanese specialties include deep-fried chicken wrapped in paper, Carp with Hot Bean Sauce, and Szechwan Duck, a cousin to the more famous Peking Duck.

Of course none of these cuisines has stayed strictly in its place. Just as Californians make their own version of southern fried chicken (though few from Alabama would recognize it), cooks in China exchange recipes.

Actually, that's not quite accurate. Recipes seem to be a Western invention. No Chinese cook worth his soy sauce ever writes anything down. For this book I often had to watch a chef prepare a dish, go home and recreate it, then go back to watch again before composing the recipe. The Chinese cook by feel, taste, experience, instinct, the seat of their pants—everything but recipes.

To them, cooking is simply a matter of perfecting certain techniques and applying them to whatever ingredients are freshest and most appealing. It's a style of cooking that is both adaptable and individualistic. You'll find recipes in this book that may at first glance seem quite similar, but the interpretations of different chefs make them completely different. You may like one version better than another, or, if you are as creative as the cooks of

China, you will use the recipe merely as a base from which to launch your own experiments, making each dish truly your own.

Now, before joining me on this gastronomic stroll through San Francisco's Chinatown, you may want to glance through the following cram course on Chinese cooking techniques.

PART I

1. Get Ready, Get Set...

The most important steps in putting together a Chinese dish take place before you heat the stove. Because most of the cooking is done very quickly (thereby conserving energy, a fact worth noting these days), all of the ingredients must be ready and at hand when the moment of truth arrives. I find it useful to line up all the ingredients in their order of appearance next to the range, so that I'm not caught fumbling through the cupboard for some long-lost oyster sauce while my beef is turning to shoe leather in the wok.

A Chinese cleaver or sharp heavy knife and a chopping block will be your best friends in the preparation of food for Chinese dishes. With only chopsticks or porcelain soup spoons in his battery of tableware, the Chinese diner depends on the chef to slice, dice, chop, sliver, and otherwise render all the ingredients into bite-size pieces before they reach the table. Small bits of food also have more exposed surfaces to absorb and exchange flavors and can be cooked quickly, preserving their natural textures.

The secret of using a cleaver effectively and safely is to hold the food down with the left hand (assuming you are right handed—if not, reverse the procedure), fingers bent under against the food and knuckles against the blade. As long as you don't lift the blade higher than your knuckles, your fingers will stay out of harm's way.

Most of the slicing techniques used in Chinese cooking are similar to those used by Western cooks. Practice will give you the confidence to turn out piles of matchstick-perfect carrot strips or paper-thin slices of flank steak. It's important to strive for uniformity. If something is cut in a small dice, then all the pieces should be the same size. This rule also applies to all the ingredients in a single dish. For instance, you wouldn't use strips of steak, chunks of green pepper, and minced mushrooms in the same dish. Not only would it look like a muddle, it would taste worse, for nothing would finish cooking at the same time.

If you enjoy Chinese food you probably already have that most versatile utensil—a wok. If you don't, consider buying one. Once you have a wok in your kitchen you'll wonder how you ever survived without it. You'll find you use it for far more than Chinese cooking. Mine comes down from its hook whenever I'm going to make beef Stroganoff, paella, scrambled eggs, or even fried chicken. However, if you aren't quite ready to invest in a wok, the recipes contained in this book can also be prepared in a heavy skillet.

If you are about to buy a wok, try to find one made of heavy iron, the traditional material. Although this type must be seasoned (the manufacturer's instructions will explain how to do this), it will last longer and distribute heat more evenly during its lifetime than will glistening stainless steel beauties. Choose a wok with a high-domed cover to multiply its uses. With the cover on it can act as a braiser or steamer.

The wok's shape, with its flared sides and rounded bottom, has remained intact for centuries, and was originally dictated by the open cylinders of clay or brick on which it rested. Today, metal collars adapt the round-bottomed wok for use on modern gas and electric ranges.

Successful stir-frying is not difficult if you get yourself organized before you begin and then keep a few basic rules in mind. Before putting the wok on the heat be sure you have everything at hand and that everything's cut up and ready for cooking. Line up the ingredients in logical order and half the battle's won.

Now, place the wok over high heat. When it is hot enough to cause a drop of water to sizzle, add a necklace of oil (peanut or corn oil are best) around the top rim of the pan so it will slither down the sides and coat the surface. In a few seconds the oil will begin to smoke. At that instant add any flavoring ingredients such as garlic, ginger, and chili peppers, stirring constantly so they will release their perfumes and flavors without burning. Next, add the remaining ingredients in order of their cooking times. Usually this will mean cooking the meat first, removing it from the wok while stir-frying the vegetables, and then adding the meat once again for a final toss over the heat. Add any liquids and thickening at this point and swirl them about to coat all the ingredients.

The term *stir-frying* doesn't precisely describe the motion used. Perhaps "toss-frying" would be closer to the mark. The process actually requires a kind of folding action using a large flat spoon or spatula. Dip it under the food and turn, keeping the whole mass in constant motion. It sounds like a messy operation, but the wok's design keeps the food from escaping as you toss it about.

Through all this it's important to remember who's in charge here. If you find yourself in a panic and things seem to be getting ahead of you, remove the wok from the heat, recoup your strength with a sip of wine, and when you've regained your poise and resolve, pick up the process where you left off. Any Chinese chef would be appalled by this unorthodox suggestion, but just knowing that you *can* stop will probably give you the confidence you need to sail through the whole thing without a hitch. With practice and experience you'll develop your stir-frying skill until only natural modesty will prevent you from showing off in front of guests.

In a Chinese kitchen a bamboo steamer does much of the work accomplished by ovens in the West. These steamers can be stacked in many layers on a wok and a whole meal prepared over a single heat source. A makeshift but quite effective steamer can be made of a large covered kettle or Dutch oven. The steam must be able to waft around the dish you are preparing, so set it in a small bowl. Place the bowl on a round cake rack or a foil pie-plate with holes punched in it, supported by two empty tuna cans with both ends cut off. The rack should be about 1½-2 inches above the inch-deep water in the pot.

With just these simple tools and techniques at your command, you can explore all the nuances of one of the world's great cuisines.

2. Shopping Notes

If you live near a Chinese community, you'll soon discover that half the fun of Chinese cooking is in rummaging through exotic markets searching for ingredients. If you lack a nearby oriental neighborhood, you'll find some provisions in your supermarket and some can be ordered by mail from one of the suppliers listed at the end of this section. If you want to try a particular recipe and can't locate one of the ingredients, remember what the Chinese would do: improvise, substitute.

The following ingredients are those most commonly found in Chinese recipes.

ANISE, STAR: These dry, brown, star-shaped "flowers" are imported from China and have a distinctive licorice flavor. They will keep indefinitely in a tightly covered container. You can substitute anise extract, but use a light hand.

BAMBOO SHOOTS: Ivory-colored shoots of tropical bamboo plants are available both fresh and canned. If fresh, the bamboo shoots must be parboiled for 15 minutes. If you are using the canned variety, be sure they're not salted. Kohlrabi or celery hearts can be substituted for texture, but the flavor will be different.

BEAN SPROUTS: Actually, these are the sprouts of tiny mung beans and are sold fresh or canned. Keep fresh sprouts in a closed plastic bag in the refrigerator. If you find you like the flavor of bean sprouts (they are a great addition to salads and omelets as well as Chinese dishes), you can grow your own.

Wash 1 cup dried mung beans and soak them overnight in 4 cups

6

water. Drain the beans and put them on a flat woven mat or a tray covered with several layers of burlap or kitchen towels. Saturate with water, pouring off any excess. Put tray in a dark place with a constant temperature of 68° to 70°. Water daily when the top dries out. The beans will sprout in 2-3 days and will be ready to harvest in 5-7 days when they are a little over an inch long.

AGAR-AGAR: A dried form of seaweed that comes in long, thin white strips.

BOK CHOY: A leafy green cabbage with white stems. It's sold either by the cluster or the heart. Substitute celery cabbage or romaine lettuce.

BROWN BEAN SAUCE: A thick sauce made from fermented yellow beans, flour, and salt. Substitute Bovril.

CHINESE CABBAGE or CELERY CABBAGE: Often called nappa cabbage, this vegetable has crisp, tightly packed stalks and is popular for soups and stir-fried dishes. Substitute savoy cabbage, young celery, lettuce, or spinach.

CHINESE PARSLEY or CORIANDER: An aromatic herb with a sharp, tangy flavor and lacy leaves. Sold fresh by the bunch in Chinese, Italian, and Latin American grocery stores.

CLOUD EARS: These small, dark brown, crinkly fungi double their size when soaked. No substitute.

FIVE SPICES: This combination of five ground spices is sold already mixed in Chinese markets. Substitute allspice.

GINGER ROOT: A gnarled, aromatic brown root, this is a basic flavor for most Chinese dishes. Ginger juice is made by cutting a piece of root in slivers, which are then squeezed in a garlic press to extract the liquid.

HOISIN SAUCE: This sauce has a sharp, spicy, but slightly sweet flavor that comes from a combination of soybeans, spices, garlic, and chili. Hoisin sauce is sold in 1-pound cans and can be stored for several months in the refrigerator in a tightly sealed container. No substitute.

LILY BUDS or GOLDEN NEEDLES: Dried, pale gold tiger lily buds are often used in the same dish with cloud ears. They must be soaked for 30 minutes to an hour before using. No substitute.

MUSHROOMS, DRIED CHINESE or FOREST: Brownish black, strongly flavored mushrooms that expand when soaked. They can be stored indefinitely at room temperature. If you substitute European dried mushrooms the flavor will be different, though equally pleasant.

MUSTARD GREENS, PICKLED: This vegetable is quite popular in Shanghai and Ningpo. The mustard greens must be thoroughly rinsed before using. Substitute rinsed sauerkraut.

OIL, COOKING: The Chinese favor peanut oil for cooking, although corn oil will do. Butter or olive oil give the wrong flavor.

OYSTER SAUCE: A thick, brownish liquid made from oysters, soy sauce, and brine. Sold in bottles and cans, it keeps indefinitely. No substitute.

PEAS, SNOW: Chinese pea pods are much daintier than our garden varieties. They are eaten pods and all, adding crisp emphasis and color to many dishes. Frozen will do if fresh are not available.

PEPPER, CHINESE RED: Aromatic red flakes, used for seasoning hot dishes. Substitute Tabasco sauce.

PEPPER, SZECHWAN: Mildly hot pepper that is pungent and aromatic. It resembles the black peppercorn but contains a small seed that provides its unique tang.

PEPPERS, CHILI: Green chili peppers are used primarily in Szechwanese cooking.

PLUM SAUCE: Traditionally served with Peking Duck, this chutney-like condiment is also used as an accompanying dip for other foods. To make your own version as a substitute for the prepared variety, see p. 83.

RICE: This is the single most important ingredient in Chinese cooking. It is the canvas on which all the other flavors of the meal

are painted. The proper preparation of Chinese rice is not difficult, though perhaps slightly different from the way you ordinarily
cook it:

Rice triples in volume when it is cooked. Allow about ½ cup
uncooked rice per person for a Chinese meal. Generally speaking,
½ cup rice absorbs 1 cup water, but some rice absorbs more and
some less, so use your judgment.

To make 2-3 servings, rinse 1 cup long or medium grain rice in
several changes of water. Place rice in a heavy pan with a tight lid
and add 1½-2 cups cold water.

Set pan over high heat and boil rapidly, uncovered, until most of
the water has been absorbed. Stir often as the water boils to
prevent the rice from sticking.

Reduce the heat to low (if you have an electric range, you may
want to use an asbestos mat to achieve a low even heat). Cover and
allow the rice to steam for 20-30 minutes. No peeking!

RICE STICK NOODLES: Thin, transluscent noodles that explode
into a froth of crisp, airy threads when deep-fried. No substitute.

SESAME SEED OIL: This expensive, golden oil has a strong,
nutty flavor and is sold in bottles in oriental markets. Just a drop
or two will season a dish, for it is highly concentrated. Don't
confuse it with the mild sesame oil sold in supermarkets.

SOY SAUCE: A tangy, salty, brown liquid made from fermented
soybeans, wheat, yeast, and salt. There are many types and grades
imported from China and Japan. Chinese soy sauce is available in
light, black, and heavy types. Unless otherwise specified, a
medium Chinese soy sauce, *chan yow*, or Japanese *shoyu* are
suggested for use in these recipes.

VINEGAR, RICE WINE: There are three types of rice vinegar:
red, white, and black. Substitute American white vinegar.

WATER CHESTNUTS: These crisp nuggets are the aquatic bulbs
of an Asian marsh plant. The fresh ones must be washed and
peeled. Also available canned. Substitute jicama or other crisp
vegetables such as celery or cabbage hearts.

SOURCES OF CHINESE FOOD AND EQUIPMENT

(All of the following suppliers will accept mail orders.)

WEST

Chong Imports
838 Grant Avenue
San Francisco, California 94108

Wo Kee & Company
949 Grant Avenue
San Francisco, California 94108

Ginn Wall Company
1016 Grant Avenue
San Francisco, California 94133
(Write for free brochure)

Shing Chong & Co.
800 Grant Avenue
San Francisco, California 94108

Gim Fat Company
953 Grant Avenue
San Francisco, California 94108

Manley Produce
1101 Grant Avenue
San Francisco, California 94113

Wing Chong Lung Co.
922 South San Pedro Street
Los Angeles, California 90015

Wah Young Company
717 South King
Seattle, Washington 98104

House of Rice
4112 University Way N.E.
Seattle, Washington 98105

SOUTH

Adler's Fine Foods
2014 Broadway
San Antonio, Texas 78215

Oriental Import-Export Co.
2009 Polk Street
Houston, Texas 77003

MIDWEST

Kam Shing Co.
2246 South Wentworth Street
Chicago, Illinois 60616

Siam
4634-36 North Lincoln Avenue
Chicago, Illinois 60625

Shiroma
1058 West Argyle Street
Chicago, Illinois 60640

Star Market
3349 North Clark Street
Chicago, Illinois 60657

New Siam
1058-60 West Argyle Avenue
Chicago, Illinois 60640

Sam Wah Yick Kee
2146 Rockwell Avenue
Cleveland, Ohio 44114

EAST

See Sun Company
36 Harrison Avenue
Boston, Massachusetts 02111

Tuck Cheon Company
617 H Street N.W.
Washington, D.C. 20001

Sun Sun Company
34a Oxford Street
Boston, Massachusetts 02111

Wing Wing Imported Groceries
79 Harrison Avenue
Boston, Massachusetts 02111

Yuet Hing Market Inc.
23 Pell Street
New York, New York 10013

East Wind
2801 Broadway
New York, New York 10025

Wing Fat Company, Inc.
35 Mott Street
New York, New York 10013

Mee Wah Lung Company
608 H Street N.W.
Washington, D.C. 20001

Wang's Company
800 Seventh Street N.W.
Washington, D.C. 20001

3. Designing a Chinese Meal

Food is a serious business in China, where the composition of a meal is considered as much a work of art as a poem or a painting. A well-planned Chinese menu appeals to all the senses with contrasts of colors, textures, flavors, and aromas. The Chinese would never consider having a single main dish as we do in the West, for it wouldn't excite their taste buds with the challenge of variety.

The rule for planning a Chinese meal, whether at home or in a restaurant, is to provide one dish for every diner. These will be shared by everyone, allowing people to switch from one taste to another as the spirit moves them. For example, if you select a delicate Winter Melon Soup, its subtlety would be pointed up by a dish of Velvet Chicken and crisp pea pods, a fragrant steamed fish, crunchy stir-fried vegetables, and a platter of spicy hot beef. Different cooking methods, different ingredients, and contrasting flavors and textures all add interest to the meal.

While this is a splendid plan for restaurant dining, it places a heavy burden on the home cook, especially one not experienced in Chinese cooking. For that reason I've given the number of servings for each recipe both as a Western main course or as a part of a Chinese menu. If a dish is to serve as a single entrée it will feed fewer people than if it is one of several dishes in a Chinese-style menu. It's a good idea to work your way through these recipes one at a time, sharpening your skills as you go along, before attempting a full-scale Chinese feast.

Tea is the traditional accompaniment to Chinese food, at least in this country. In China, tea is more commonly sipped on and off during the day and at the close of a meal. Whenever it appears, its preparation is a ritual combining art with tradition. The Chinese feel that spring water is ideal for steeping the tea leaves and that it is best brewed in an earthenware pot. It is said that the Dowager Empress was such a perfectionist that she had her tea prepared with early-morning dew gathered in marble vessels by her ladies-in-waiting.

Wine is generally reserved for banquets in China, and, like saki, is often served warm. Most Chinese wines, as they are distilled from rice and other grains, are really more like our liqueurs and whisky. Some contain staggering amounts of alcohol. A recent import from China, *Chefoo,* is made from grapes. It is slightly sweet and similar to a light port.

Most wine fanciers feel that a fruity, moderately dry white wine best accompanies Chinese food, with rosé a second choice. Although it is not authentic to serve Western table wines with a Chinese meal, it's a pleasant improvisation. Personally, I'm very fond of beer with Chinese food. (To tell the truth, I'm very fond of beer, period, so I suppose that colors my thinking. However, it seems to me that some of the spicier dishes from Hunan and Szechwan fairly compel the quaffing of a cold brew.)

No matter what you choose to drink with your Chinese meal, the food is the main attraction. So come with me and we'll sneak through some kitchen doors to find out how San Francisco's finest Chinese chefs prepare it.

PART II

4. Restaurants and Their Recipes

ASIA GARDEN
772 Pacific Avenue
415-398-5112

Whenever I have an hour to spare and feel the urge for a quick trip to Hong Kong, I hike up Pacific Avenue and step into Asia Garden. The voices of the pretty girls singing out the names of the dishes they carry on their trolleys instantly takes me back to a *dim sum* lunch I had in Hong Kong with my friends Merle and Nisbert Kwong. I remember Nisbert patiently explaining the ingredients of every dish while I viewed and then sampled an immoderate assortment. We ate for hours before tottering out into the humid Hong Kong afternoon. I vowed never to eat again. Of course the Kwongs saw to it that I broke my pledge that very evening—but that's another story.

Asia Garden is a replica of that restaurant of my memory, a sprawling room filled with ever-changing patterns of people, lusty conversations being conducted in several languages, and tantalizing smells filling the air. Shelton Chang, who manages the restaurant with precision and care, orchestrates the feeding of over fifteen hundred people a day here. It's a job that would send most mess-hall sergeants over the hill, and what makes the undertaking even more staggering is that all the *dim sum* specialties must be made by hand.

I had the chance to visit the kitchen, which is only a little smaller than the Astrodome, with acres of immaculate stainless steel and teams of cooks working under the direction of chef Sum Yu. In one corner I watched a group preparing thousands of *Shoa-mai*, the pork-filled dumplings whose shape has always reminded me of perky nurse-caps. One young man in a single swift movement of the

15

heel of his hand flattened a ball of dough into a perfect round. Another person added the filling, while several facile-fingered workers folded and pleated the dumplings with the precision of Swiss watchmakers.

Those same dumplings, along with many other Asia Garden specialties, can be purchased in the restaurant lobby by those who want something to take home to tide them over until their next visit. I always stock up, smug in the knowledge that I'm putting off for a while longer that inevitable—and expensive—round-trip ticket to Hong Kong.

BAKED BARBECUED PORK BUNS

Chinese breads are more often steamed than baked, but Asia Garden chef Sum Yu has perfected this delicate baked bun. I think they're best with tea as an afternoon snack, but they also can add an original touch to a breakfast or brunch menu.

DOUGH
1 package dry yeast	**2 cups flour**
1 cup warm water	**1 tablespoon sugar**
1 tablespoon oil	**⅛ teaspoon salt**

FILLING
⅔ pound barbecued pork (see p. 91)	**6 green onions, chopped fine**

GLAZE
2 tablespoons warm water	**1 teaspoon oil**
1 teaspoon sugar	

Sprinkle the dry yeast over the lukewarm water in a bowl. Stir until the yeast has dissolved. Add the oil and stir again. Place flour, sugar, and salt in a sifter and gradually sift dry ingredients into liquid, mixing well with a wooden spoon after each addition. The dough will be quite rubbery at this point. Beat for another 5 minutes with the spoon until the dough is smooth and springy. Form into a ball and cover with a damp dishcloth. Allow the dough to rise in a warm place for about 2 hours or until it has doubled in volume.

Preheat oven to 450°. Punch down the raised dough and knead it on a lightly floured surface just until smooth. Pinch off 12-15 pieces of dough about the size of a giant walnut or an undernourished egg. Roll each piece into a 4-inch round about ¼-inch thick. Mince the barbecued pork and mix with the chopped green onions. Spoon a generous tablespoon of the filling in the center of each round. Bring edges of the dough up and around the filling so that it looks something like a hobo's knapsack. Twist the edges together with your thumb and index finger to seal. Put the buns, with their smooth sides up and twisted sides down, on baking sheets; cover and allow them to rise again for 15-30 minutes.

Brush the tops of the buns with glaze mixture. Bake for about 10 minutes or until the tops are a glowing golden brown.

WHITE FLOWER DUMPLING IN GREEN PEPPER

These bite-size morsels make exotic appetizers or cocktail party fare. They'll perk up even the most jaded palate.

2 whole green peppers	1 teaspoon sesame seed oil
1 pound shrimp, finely	¼ teaspoon white pepper
minced in blender	1 tablespoon cornstarch
¼ teaspoon salt	2 tablespoons cooking oil
1 teaspoon MSG (optional)	¼ cup water
2 teaspoons sugar	

GARLIC-SOY DIPPING SAUCE
  2 cloves garlic, minced
¼ cup soy sauce

Prepare Garlic-Soy Dipping Sauce by adding 2 minced cloves garlic to ¼ cup soy sauce. Allow to stand for ½ hour before using.

Cut peppers in half and scoop out centers (do not wash them inside or filling won't stick). Cut each half again lengthwise and then crosswise. Dust inside of each pepper square with cornstarch to help filling stick.

Combine remaining ingredients and beat together for 2-3 minutes with an electric mixer.

Fill each pepper square with some shrimp mixture and pat firmly.

Heat a flat-bottomed skillet until very hot and add 2 tablespoons cooking oil, swirling it around to cover the bottom of the pan. Place filled green peppers in a single layer in the bottom of the skillet. Reduce heat to low, cover pan, and cook for 5 minutes. Add ¼ cup water, cover, and cook 5 minutes longer or until liquid has evaporated.

Serve at once with Garlic-Soy Dipping Sauce.

Makes 16 dumplings.

STEAMED PORK BALLS WITH NOODLE CASINGS

NOODLE DOUGH

1 whole egg, beaten	**2 cups flour**
¼ cup water	**½ teaspoon salt**

FILLING:

1 pound pork butt	**3 ounces pork fat**
6 dried black mushrooms, soaked in warm water for 15 minutes	**½ teaspoon salt**
	2 teaspoons sugar
½ pound raw prawns, shelled and deveined	**2 teaspoons soy sauce**
	1 teaspoon sesame seed oil

To make the dough, add the egg and water to the flour and salt and mix thoroughly with a wooden spatula or spoon. Turn dough onto a floured surface and knead until smooth. Cut off small pieces and roll into 1-inch balls. Roll or flatten into thin rounds approximately 3 inches in diameter. Dust lightly with cornstarch and stack. Cover with plastic wrap while you prepare the filling.

To make the filling, finely chop the pork, mushrooms, prawns, and pork fat. Mix the chopped ingredients together thoroughly. Stir in the salt, sugar, soy sauce, and sesame seed oil.

To assemble, place a generous teaspoon of the filling in the middle of each round wrapper. Gather the edges of the wrapper around the filling, allowing the sides to pleat naturally and leaving some of the filling exposed on the top. Squeeze the middle of the pork balls to pack the filling firmly.

To steam, use a Chinese steamer or improvise one according to the directions on page 5.

Place the Pork Balls in the steamer a few at a time, cover, and steam for 30 minutes.

Makes about 2 dozen pork balls.

NOTE: You can freeze cooked Pork Balls for as long as a month. Place them on a baking sheet and freeze until firm, then place in plastic bags and seal. When ready to serve, thaw and steam again until heated through.

CHUNG KING
606 Jackson Street
415-986-3899

Chung King is the kind of small, original restaurant that people discover and then try to keep to themselves. No wonder—the food is exciting and the prices low.

Although its name might call up a nightmare of canned noodles and *chop suey* to Americans, the city of Chungking is actually the commercial center of Szechwan and the hub of one of China's most interesting cuisines. The city is built on a picturesque rock promontory at the conjunction of the Kialing and Yangtze rivers; supplies brought to the city by river are carried up by stairway or inclined railway. Chungking is also the original home of Chi Wei Wang, owner and chef of this fascinating little restaurant.

The food of Chungking, although influenced by migrants from the north, fundamentally is the highly complex cooking style of Szechwan. Although many people are startled by the spiciness of their first taste of Szechwan cooking (a cold beer will never taste better than after your first bite of Hot Diced Chicken), a symphony of flavors remains, teasing the palate into alertness.

Among the typical dishes available at this bistrolike, brick-walled restaurant are Twice-Cooked Pork, Braised Prawns in Szechwan Sauce, General Chow's Chicken, Szechwan Cabbage, and *Sah-Chai* Beef.

Although most dishes at Chung King are well within the means of unpublished poets, three spectacular offerings demand a recent inheritance or income tax refund. For $17 you can explore the wonders of either Stewed Shark's Fin, Stewed Shark's Fin and Shredded Chicken Soup, or Three Ingredient Shark's Fin. I have yet to splurge on these sumptuous dishes, being perfectly content to continue soothing my hunger pangs with extravagant helpings of Ants Climbing a Tree.

ANTS CLIMBING A TREE

This is one of my favorite dishes, despite its rather off-putting name. One day a friend and I had lunch at Chung King and managed to devour a staggering quantity of Ants Climbing a Tree. Chi Wei Wang merely smiled at our gluttony and kept sending us more platters of lettuce leaves when we ran out.

½ pound beef (flank steak, sirloin, or filet)
½ cup water chestnuts
½ green pepper
½ cup bamboo shoots
1 tablespoon finely chopped fresh ginger
6 dried black or forest mushrooms, soaked for 30 minutes in warm water
1 tablespoon rice wine or dry sherry
1 tablespoon soy sauce
salt to taste
1 cup chicken broth
1 tablespoon cornstarch
4 tablespoons cooking oil
2-3 fresh or dried red peppers or ½ teaspoon chili oil (see p. 24)
¼ pound rice stick noodles
oil for deep frying
1 head lettuce, washed and crisped

Mince the beef until it is as fine as you think you can make it. Then mince it again. You can grind the meat, but the texture will be quite different and it's really worth the effort to do it correctly. The water chestnuts, green pepper, bamboo shoots, and ginger should be minced in the same way—until they are reduced to a fine dice. Drain the mushrooms and cut off stems. Dry them with paper towels and mince them as you have the other ingredients.

In a small bowl mix together the rice wine or sherry, soy sauce, chicken broth, and cornstarch.

If you are using dried red peppers, soak them in warm water until softened, then seed and chop them. Fresh red peppers need only seeding and chopping. If you are using chili oil, simply have it on hand.

Heat 4 tablespoons cooking oil in a wok or skillet until very hot. Add the beef and toss over high heat until it has lost its pink color. Immediately add the water chestnuts, green peppers, mushrooms, bamboo shoots, and minced ginger. Stir-fry for a minute longer.

Add the soy-broth mixture and the minced red peppers or chili oil and cook, stirring constantly, until thickened and the liquid is reduced—about 5 minutes.

Meanwhile, heat cooking oil in a pan to 365° or until oil foams around a cube of fresh bread. Add rice sticks and stir for 1-2 minutes or until noodles expand and become a pale golden color. Place noodles on a platter and spoon the meat mixture on top. When ready to serve, toss rice stick noodles with the meat mixture. The noodles are said to resemble tree bark and the tiny pieces of beef and vegetables are the ants—hence the name.

To eat, put a couple of spoonsful of the mixture on a crisp lettuce leaf, fold it over and roll it up to enclose the filling. Now pick it up and eat it with your fingers. No inhibitions are allowed.

This makes about 4 main course servings, unless I'm coming to lunch.

WHOLE CHILI FISH

1 whole striped bass, rock cod, or other firm white fish (about 2 pounds)

1 teaspoon salt
½ cup cornstarch
oil for deep-frying

CHILI SAUCE

6 dried forest mushrooms, soaked in warm water for 30 minutes
2 tablespoons oil
¼ cup bamboo shoots, cut in slivers
¼ cup chopped green onion
½ teaspoon minced fresh ginger root
1 tablespoon soy sauce
1 tablespoon brown bean sauce (Bovril may be substituted if necessary)

½ teaspoon salt
2 tablespoons dry sherry
1 tablespoon rice vinegar or white vinegar
1 teaspoon sugar
½ teaspoon chili oil (see p. 24)
1 tablespoon cornstarch mixed with 2 tablespoons water

Have the fish cleaned and scaled but left whole. Wash the fish and pat it dry with paper towels. Score fish on each side with 3 diagonally placed slashes. Sprinkle fish lightly with salt and rub it in.

Dredge fish in cornstarch until lightly coated. Heat enough oil to cover fish in a wok or skillet until it reaches 350° or foams around a cube of bread dropped into it. Gently lower the fish into the oil (if the fish spatters a great deal, cover the pan until the spattering stops) . Fry the fish, spooning oil over it, for 5-7 minutes. Turn the fish and fry on the other side for an additional 5-7 minutes or until golden. Transfer the fish to a platter and keep warm in a low oven.

Now prepare the chili sauce. Drain mushrooms and dry with paper towels. Cut off the tough stems and discard. Cut mushrooms into matchstick slivers. Heat the 2 tablespoons oil in a wok or skillet and add the mushrooms, bamboo shoots, green onions, and ginger. Cook for 1 minute, stirring and turning the ingredients. Combine the remaining ingredients, add to the wok and cook, stirring constantly until thickened. Pour sauce over the crisply fried fish and serve immediately.

Serves 2 as a main course or 4 as part of a whole Chinese meal.

HOT AND SOUR SOUP

When a damp and chilling fog comes sneaking in through the Golden Gate, San Franciscans make haste to Chung King for a bowl of this hearty, soul-satisfying soup.

6 dried forest mushrooms, soaked in warm water for 30 minutes	**1 tablespoon soy sauce**
	¼ teaspoon white pepper
2 squares fresh Chinese bean curd, about 3-inches square by ½-inch thick	**1 tablespoon rice wine or dry sherry**
	2 tablespoons rice vinegar or white vinegar
½ cup canned bamboo shoots	**salt to taste**
¼ cup water chestnuts	**2 tablespoons cornstarch mixed with 3 tablespoons cold water**
½ cup cloud ears, soaked in warm water for 30 minutes	
¼ pound lean pork	**1 egg, beaten**
1 quart chicken broth, fresh or canned	**2 teaspoons sesame seed oil**
	2 tablespoons chopped green onion

**1 teaspoon minced ginger root   ½ teaspoon chili oil
                                        (optional)***

Drain the mushrooms and pat dry. Cut off the tough stems and discard. Shred the caps by cutting horizontally into paper-thin slices and then into slender strips.

Drain bean curd and bamboo shoots and rinse them under cold water. Shred them until they are the same shape as the mushrooms. Sliver the water chestnuts in a similar fashion. Rinse cloud ears and rub between your fingers to remove any grit. Cut into slivers.

Trim pork of all fat and then cut it into slivers about 2 inches long.

Have all the ingredients ready and within easy reach when you begin preparing the soup.

In a heavy pot combine the chicken broth, ginger root, soy sauce, pork, mushrooms, bamboo shoots, water chestnuts, and cloud ears. Bring to a boil over high heat, reduce heat to low and simmer, covered, for 10 minutes. Drop in the bean curd and add the pepper, rice wine or sherry, and vinegar. Add salt to taste. Bring the soup back to a boil. Stir the cornstarch mixture to blend, then add to the soup, stirring constantly. When the soup has thickened, remove from the heat and add the beaten egg, stirring rapidly. Add the green onions, sesame seed oil, and chili oil. Stir well and serve immediately.

Serves 4-6.

---

*Chili Oil: This fiery condiment is available bottled in Chinese markets. To make your own, heat 1 cup peanut oil until it begins to smoke. Remove from the heat and add ¼ cup cayenne pepper or powdered red pepper. Stir well. Cool and store in a glass jar. Tabasco (hot pepper) sauce may be substituted.

THE DYNASTY
3317 Steiner
415-563-7779

In recent years more and more exciting Chinese restaurants have sprouted far from the bustle of San Francisco's Chinatown. One of my favorites, the Dynasty, is located in the quiet Marina district. The combination of first-rate food and handsome decor makes it popular with young couples, who cheerfully give up hand-holding when their meal arrives to devote their full attention to the delights of the table.

A jolly laughing Buddha at the entrance sets the tone for this restaurant, where eating is a happy adventure. The Dynasty specializes in both northern Chinese and Szechwanese cooking (two types that are often inexplicably combined on menus in this country). While northern Chinese food is light, elegant, and delicate in flavor, with a discreet use of garlic, scallions, and chives, Szechwanese cooking is highly spiced, peppery, and rather oily. In the mountainous inland province of Szechwan, the scorching summer temperatures dictate equally torrid food. I have never fully understood this phenomenon, but a glance at the cuisines of India, Mexico, and other hot countries confirms that the instinct to counter soaring temperatures with searing food is universal.

The vigorous flavor of Szechwan pepper, or *fagara*, western Chinese cooking's most distinctive ingredient, is positively unforgettable. This pepper has mysterious properties that numb the mouth for a moment before it launches a full-scale assault. Then all at once the pepper takes hold, strong and hot, but also in some way stimulating the palate to appreciate the subtleties of sour, salty, sweet, and bitter all at once. Szechwan pepper is not for the fainthearted, but its properties are exciting and invigorating to those with a spirit of adventure.

If you cannot buy Szechwan peppercorns in your area, you can still try the two Dynasty recipes that call for it by substituting red pepper flakes or Tabasco sauce. They won't be quite authentic, but they'll still wake up your mouth.

PORK À LA SZECHWAN

You might assume from the name of this dish that it came to San Francisco by way of Paris, but I can assure you its breathtaking peppery flavor is pure Szechwanese.

1 pound pork

BATTER

1 egg	**½ teaspoon salt**
4 tablespoons flour	**2-4 tablespoons water**

SAUCE

4 green onions	**2 tablespoons rice wine vinegar**
3 cloves garlic, minced or	**or cider vinegar**
mashed	**1 teaspoon sugar**
2-3 slices fresh ginger root,	**½ teaspoon crushed red pepper**
minced	**flakes or ground Szechwan**
1 tablespoon dry sherry	**peppercorns or Tabasco sauce**
2 tablespoons soy sauce	**oil for deep-frying**
1 teaspoon tomato paste	

Cut pork (pork butt is an excellent cut to use for this dish) into ¾-1-inch cubes. Mix together batter ingredients in a bowl and beat until thoroughly mixed.

Cut green onions into ¼ inch slices. Mince or mash garlic and ginger slices. Combine sherry, soy sauce, vinegar, tomato paste, sugar, and red pepper flakes or ground peppercorns or Tabasco in a small bowl. Have these ingredients ready before beginning to cook pork.

Heat oil in wok or deep-fryer to 375°. Coat pork cubes with batter. Deep-fry pork cubes a few at a time in the oil until golden brown (about 8 minutes). Drain pork thoroughly on paper towels and keep warm while preparing the sauce.

Pour off all but 2 tablespoons of the oil from the wok. Add green onions, garlic, and ginger. Stir-fry for 1-2 minutes. Pour in the sherry-soy mixture and cook for 2-3 minutes. Add deep-fried pork pieces and stir briefly to coat with sauce. Serve at once.

Serves 3-4 as a main dish or 6 as part of a full Chinese menu.

MANCHURIAN BEEF

1 pound lean beef (sirloin,
   tenderloin, flank, or round
   steak)

MARINADE
1 egg white   ½ teaspoon salt
1 tablespoon cornstarch

BATTER
  1 egg   2 tablespoons water
  2 tablespoons flour   ½ teaspoon salt
oil for deep-frying   2 tablespoons soy sauce
  2 green onions, minced   1 teaspoon sugar
1-2 slices ginger root, minced   1½ teaspoons sesame seed oil
  2 tablespoons dry sherry

Cut the beef across the grain into paper-thin slices (you'll find this easier if the meat is slightly frozen). Pound slices even thinner with a mallet or the side of a cleaver and cut into ½-by 1½-inch pieces.

Mix together the marinade ingredients in a bowl. Add beef and toss gently. Let stand for an hour, turning meat occasionally.

Drain meat and blot it dry with paper towels. Mix together the batter ingredients in a bowl. Add beef and toss gently until coated.

Pour cooking oil in a wok or skillet to a depth of 2 inches. Heat oil to 375° or until it foams around a bread cube. Add beef, a small amount at a time, and fry until brown (1-2 minutes). Remove beef and drain on paper towels.

Pour off oil from wok or skillet and return pan to the heat. When pan is hot again, add minced green onion and minced ginger and stir-fry briefly. Add sherry, soy sauce, sugar, and sesame seed oil. When sauce is very hot, return beef to pan and stir to coat beef with the sauce.

Serves 2 as a main course with rice or 4-6 on a complete Chinese menu.

KING PO SHRIMP

The Dynasty's fragile deep-fried shrimp slip into a sauce with real authority.

6 **water chestnuts**	2 **tablespoons cider vinegar**
2 **thin slices ginger**	**or rice vinegar**
4 **cloves garlic**	1 **teaspoon salt**
½ **cup bamboo shoots**	1½ **teaspoons cornstarch**
2 **tablespoons wood ears**	1 **tablespoon water**
(optional)	½ **teaspoon crushed red pepper**
3 **green onions**	**flakes or ground Szechwan**
2 **tablespoons dry white wine**	**peppercorns or a few drops**
or dry sherry	**Tabasco sauce**
2 **tablespoons soy sauce**	1 **pound shrimp**
1½ **teaspoons sugar**	

BATTER

4 **tablespoons flour**	1 **egg**
½ **teaspoon salt**	2-4 **tablespoons water**

oil for deep-frying
2 **teaspoons sesame seed oil**

Mince water chestnuts, ginger, and garlic. Cut drained and rinsed bamboo shoots into slivers. Rinse wood ears and cover with warm water. Soak at least 30 minutes. Rinse again under cold water and rub between your fingers to remove grit and twigs. Cut into slivers. Cut green onions in half lengthwise and then into 1-inch pieces.

Combine wine, soy sauce, sugar, vinegar, and salt in a small bowl. Mix cornstarch with water in another small bowl. Have all these ingredients and the crushed red pepper or substitute arranged near the stove before you begin to prepare the shrimp.

Shell and devein shrimp. Combine the batter ingredients in a bowl and add shrimp. Stir to cover them with batter. Heat oil in wok or deep-fryer until it reaches 375° or until it foams around a bread cube. Remove shrimp from batter with a slotted spoon and drop in oil one at a time (if you drop them in all at once they'll cling together in a stubborn mass), or place shrimp in a wire basket and lower into the oil. Deep-fry shrimp until golden (about 3-5 minutes). Remove and drain. Keep the shrimp warm while preparing the rest of the dish.

Remove all but 2 tablespoons of oil from the wok. Heat oil until very hot. Add water chestnuts, ginger, garlic, bamboo shoots, wood ears, green onions, and crushed red pepper flakes, Szechwan pepper or Tabasco. Stir-fry briefly (1-2 minutes). Stir in prepared wine-soy sauce mixture, then cornstarch mixture, and cook for 2-3 minutes until the sauce has thickened. Stir in deep-fried shrimp and sesame seed oil and stir to combine with sauce. Serve immediately.
Serves 3 as a main dish or 6 as part of a full Chinese meal.

CHICKEN FILET SAUTÉED

This delicate Dynasty specialty is a splendid counterpoint to some of the spicier dishes offered on the menu.

1 chicken breast, skinned, boned, and cut lengthwise into ¼-inch strips

MARINADE

1 egg white, lightly beaten
1 tablespoon dry sherry
1 cup snow peas, fresh or frozen and thawed
½ cup bamboo shoots
3 tablespoons oil

½ teaspoon salt
1 slice fresh ginger root
1 clove garlic
¼ cup chicken broth
salt

Mix marinade ingredients together. Toss chicken slices in mixture and marinate for 15-20 minutes.

Stem and string snow peas if fresh. If using fresh bamboo shoots, pare and parboil them for 15 minutes, then shred. Place wok or skillet over high heat and add 2 tablespoons oil. When oil is very hot add ginger slice and garlic clove to the pan. Cook briefly to flavor the oil and remove. Add chicken strips and stir-fry for 2-3 minutes. Remove chicken from the pan.

Add remaining tablespoon of oil to the pan and add snow peas and bamboo shoots. Stir-fry about 1 minute. Add chicken broth, cover, and steam for 1 minute. Return chicken to the pan, add salt to taste, and cook, stirring, 1 minute longer.

Serve immediately to 2 as a single course or 4 as part of a complete Chinese menu.

EMPRESS OF CHINA
838 Grant Avenue (near Washington)
415-434-1345

Perched like a perfect jewel in a Tiffany setting, the Empress of China sits serenely six floors above the color and clamor of San Francisco's famed Grant Avenue. Stepping off the elevator into the Empress Pavilion is like walking into a tranquil garden. The octagonal wood pavilion was inspired by one in the former royal pleasure park in Peking and shelters a gnarled pine tree surrounded by banks of brightly blooming flowers.

The 50-ton pavilion was carved in Taiwan by a descendant of palace craftsmen, then shipped to San Francisco and reassembled without the use of a single nail. Such passion for detail is evident throughout the restaurant.

Searching for just the right atmosphere, the founders of the Empress of China researched Chinese architectural styles until they settled on one that was ideal for their purposes—that of the Han Dynasty (206 B.C.). The muted jade greens and quiet elegance of the decor is a reflection of that period.

The menu is equally sophisticated, offering something for all tastes. Regional delicacies such as Manchurian Beef, Shanghai Kuo-tieh, Szechwan Spice Beef, Mongolian Hundred Blossom Lamb, Barbecued Young Quail, Whole Winter Melon Soup, Sizzling Rice Soup, North China Onion Bread, Flaming Sweets, and Honey Apple appear on the daily menu. Peking Duck, whose golden-lacquered skin is a treat for all tastebuds, is only one of the many methods of preparing duck here. Pi Pa Duck, a less familiar dish, was introduced in the Han era by Lady Huang Chao Jiun, one of China's great beauties who was an accomplished performer on the *pi pa,* an ancient version of the modern Western guitar.

The Empress of China's chef, Lui Foon, a native of Kwantung province, is from a family of chefs, many of whom served at the royal court in Peking. He presides over a corps of chefs who perform on a 71-foot Chinese wok-oven-range that is the largest such arrangement in the country.

Luckily, we need no such elaborate equipment to recreate some of the Empress of China's most popular dishes at home.

WHOLE WINTER MELON SOUP

This elegant soup is cooked and served in its own beautiful green melon shell. If you have no local purveyor of Chinese produce, you'll have to be satisfied with reading the recipe and tasting it in your imagination until you can visit San Francisco and sample the real thing at the Empress of China.

1 winter melon, 8-8½ inches in diameter, 10-12 inches tall
⅓ cup tender bamboo shoots (canned), diced
⅓ cup small, whole, young button mushrooms
¾ cup parboiled green peas

⅓ cup dried lotus seeds (or substitute slivered blanched almonds)
10 ounces fresh white chicken meat, diced
chicken broth
salt

OPTIONAL
⅓ cup dried black mushrooms   **½ cup diced smoked ham**
⅓ cup gingko nuts

Wash the melon and scrub the outside skin until the white powder on it is removed. Cut off the top 3 inches of the melon to form a lid. Scoop out seeds and pulp and scrape inside surface clean. Wash in cold water.

Place the melon upright in a large 4-6 inch deep heatproof dish to support the melon while cooking and serving. Into the prepared melon place bamboo shoots, mushrooms, lotus seeds, chicken meats, and, if you wish, optional ingredients. Pour in chicken broth to fill ¾ of the melon. Cover with melon lid. Place the dish-supported whole melon in a wide, tall pot. Place a small rack between the cooking dish and the bottom of the pot for protection of the dish and to aid in steaming. Pour in 3-4 inches of hot water to generate steam during cooking.

Cover pot, steam melon over low heat for 3-4 hours until translucent and tender but still firm (the length of time is determined by the size and age of the melon). Add hot water to pot after the first hour for continuous steaming action.

During the last 10 minutes of cooking, add ¾ cup parboiled green peas, salt to taste, and additional chicken broth to fill the melon up to the original ¾ level mark.

Keep the melon in the large pot until ready to serve, then carefully remove the steaming whole melon with its supporting dish and place on table. To serve, ladle soup into individual bowls with some of the ingredients and bits of the melon meat. Sensational! *Serves 6-8.*

EMPRESS SPICED BEEF

This peppery dish originated in Szechwan province, the hot interior region with a reputation for highly spiced foods.

½ **pound flank steak**	**1 tablespoon and 1 cup oil**
1 medium green pepper	**1 tablespoon cornstarch**
¼ **medium onion**	**1 teaspoon soy sauce**
2 ounces Jar-Choy (spiced preserved Chinese mustard greens)	**4 drops sesame seed oil**
	pinch salt
1 hot green pepper	½ **teaspoon hot pepper sauce (Tabasco)**
1 egg	

THICKENING MIXTURE (Mix together and set aside)

1 tablespoon soy sauce	¼ **cup cold water**
salt and pepper	**2 tablespoons Chinese rice wine or dry sherry**
½ **teaspoon sugar**	
1 tablespoon cornstarch	

Slice the flank steak, green pepper, onion, Jar-Choy, and hot green pepper into long, thin slices. Beat the egg and place half of the beaten egg in a bowl (reserve remaining egg for other recipes). To egg add 1 tablespoon oil, soy sauce, sesame seed oil, salt, and pepper sauce. Dredge sliced beef in cornstarch, add to the egg mixture, and let stand 10 minutes.

Pour 1 cup cooking oil in a wok or heavy skillet.When oil is sizzling hot, toss in the prepared beef and quickly stir-fry until nearly done (about 1 minute). Remove meat from pan.

Stir in sliced green pepper, onion, Jar-Choy, and hot green pepper. Stir-fry briefly, drain off all but 3 tablespoons of oil.

Return meat to pan and add thickening mixture. Stir-fry quickly to heat everything through and until sauce thickens. Serve immediately.

Serves 2 as a main course or 4-6 as one course of a full Chinese meal.

PI PA DUCK

This court dish of the Han era is featured in special Empress of China banquets.

4-5 pound duck, thoroughly cleaned
1 cup *Min-see* (ground bean sauce)
1 cup *Nam-yui* (red bean curd)
1 tablespoon Chinese rice wine or dry sherry

1 teaspoon sugar
2 green onions, finely chopped
3 small slices fresh ginger, finely chopped
½ cup honey
Chinese parsley

Thoroughly dry the duck inside and out by patting with paper towels. Put *Min-see, Nam-yui*, wine, sugar, onions, and ginger in a bowl and mix thoroughly. Place the duck in the marinade, making sure the cavity is filled with the sauce. Cover and refrigerate for 1 hour, turning often.

Remove duck from the marinade and hang to dry for 3-4 hours. Spread honey lightly on the duck's skin (a brush works well for this).

Turn oven to 325° (do not preheat). Place duck, breast side up, on rack in roasting pan and place in the middle rack of the oven. Roast 15 minutes. Turn duck breast side down and roast another 15 minutes. Cover wings and legs with foil and remove accumulated fat from the pan with a bulb baster. Reduce heat to 250° and roast breast side up 30 minutes. Turn again and roast breast side down for 30 minutes. Turn heat up to 350° and roast breast side up 15-30 minutes or until skin is crisp and dry. Do not prick or baste duck during cooking. Remove duck from the oven and allow to stand for 15 minutes. With a cleaver, chop duck into bite-size pieces (bones and all) and garnish with sprigs of Chinese parsley.

Serves 4 as a single course or 6 in a full menu.

EMPRESS BEEF

3 tablespoons cooking oil	**1 small can button mushrooms,**
½ pound sirloin steak, cut	**thinly sliced**
into shoestring strips	**¼ teaspoon salt**
3 stalks celery, coarsely	**½ small can water chestnuts,**
chopped	**drained and thinly sliced**
1 large white onion, thinly	**¼ pound snow peas, each piece**
sliced	**cut in half on the diagonal**

THICKENING MIXTURE (Mix together and set aside)
1 tablespoon cornstarch   **2 teaspoons sugar**
5 tablespoons Chinese soy   **½ cup water**
sauce

Heat oil in a wok or skillet until very hot. Add salt and beef. Stir-fry briefly and add celery, onion, mushrooms, water chestnuts, and snow peas. Stir-fry briefly over a hot fire. Cover pan, turn down heat, and simmer for about 3 minutes. Just before serving, stir in the thickening mixture and cook quickly over high heat. Serve immediately with fluffy steamed rice.

Serves 2-3 as a main course with rice or 4-6 as one dish in a full Chinese menu.

FOUR SEAS

731 Grant Avenue
415-397-5577

Four Seas is a quiet oasis in the midst of Chinatown. With its restrained decor and calm pace, it has the atmosphere of a private club. One almost expects to see an oriental version of Lord Peter Wimsey dining here. Certainly Bunter, his butler, would approve of the impeccably starched linen and the intricately folded napkins on the tables.

Under your feet you'll find a handsome carpet with a design of Chinese junks woven into the wine red background. A screen covered with Chinese characters hides the kitchen from view and a delicate scroll depicting the Great Wall covers one end of the room.

The menu is extensive, with such specialties as Chicken Gold Coin—layers of chicken, ham, and pork served with buns; Sweet and Sour Pork with Lychees and Pineapples; Sweet Corn Boneless Chicken; and a variety of crab dishes when that tasty shellfish is in season.

I like the Four Seas' gracious gesture of providing steaming-hot towels at the end of the meal. They're especially appreciated if you've had the Butterfly Prawns. I've never successfully managed to transfer a prawn from plate to mouth with chopsticks, and long ago gave up the effort, happily and messily resorting to my fingers. Conscious of the smallest details, Four Seas doesn't sully its tables with sordid bottles of sauces. Instead, three classics—Hoisin, plum, and mustard—are arranged in pretty cloverleaf dishes.

I always leave the Four Seas feeling not only well fed, but also pleasantly pampered.

FOUR SEAS CHICKEN MUSHROOM SAUTÉ

1 frying chicken, boned	1 can medium button mush-
salt	rooms, drained
pepper	1 cup sliced bamboo shoots,
1 tablespoon gin or vodka	canned
(optional)	½ cup chicken broth
½ cup flour	2 tablespoons cornstarch
oil for deep frying	water
2 tablespoons oil	dash sesame seed oil
1 clove garlic	1 cup Chinese snow peas,
¼ cup sliced onion	lightly blanched
¼ cup sliced celery	coriander

Cut boned chicken meat into ½-inch cubes. Season lightly with salt and pepper. Brush with gin or vodka (optional) and dredge in flour.

Heat frying oil in a deep pot to 375° or until it foams around a cube of bread. Carefully immerse the chicken pieces and cook quickly until golden. Remove and drain.

Preheat skillet or wok and when very hot add 2 tablespoons of oil, a pinch of salt, and the peeled clove of garlic. Stir quickly and add the onion, celery, mushrooms, and bamboo shoots. Stir-fry for a minute or two; add chicken. Stir and toss thoroughly. Add chicken broth, cover and simmer for 2-3 minutes.

Blend the cornstarch with enough water to make a light paste. Add a dash of sesame seed oil. Add the snow peas to the skillet and cook for 30 seconds, uncovered. Add cornstarch mixture and the remaining tablespoon of oil to the skillet and stir thoroughly, cooking until the sauce is thick and glossy. Serve immediately, garnished with coriander.

Serves 4 as a single course with rice or 6-8 on a full Chinese menu.

SWEET AND SOUR PORK WITH LYCHEE AND PINEAPPLE

1 pound pork butt	1 cup pineapple chunks,
½ teaspoon MSG (optional)	drained (reserve liquid)
½ teaspoon salt	1 can lychees, drained
pinch pepper	(reserve liquid)
¼ teaspoon garlic powder	catsup
1 egg, beaten	3 tablespoons cornstarch
cracker crumbs	water
oil for deep frying	1 small green pepper, cored,
½ cup rice vinegar or white	seeded, and diced
vinegar	sesame seeds

Cut pork butt into ½-inch squares and season with MSG, if you like, and salt, pepper, and garlic powder. Dip in beaten egg and dredge in cracker crumbs.

Heat cooking oil in a deep pot to 360° or until it foams around a cube of bread. Carefully lower the dredged pork into the oil and deep-fry until brown and cooked. Remove and place on a paper towel to drain.

In a wok or skillet, mix together vinegar, ¼ cup pineapple juice, ¼ cup lychee juice, and sufficient catsup to color the sauce. Bring to a boil. Mix the cornstarch with sufficient water to form a light paste and add to the skillet or wok to thicken the sauce. Add the cooked pork squares, pineapple chunks, lychees, and green pepper and stir together. Place on a serving dish and sprinkle with sesame seeds.

Serves 2-3 as a single course or 4-6 as one of a parade of dishes on a full Chinese menu.

THE GOLDEN PAVILION
Sacramento at Grant
415-393-2334

Sitting at a window table at the Golden Pavilion is like having a ringside seat at one of the greatest shows on earth. Below on Grant Avenue, tourists limp by on blistered feet while residents pause for a bit of gossip in the middle of this crowded and narrow street that bisects San Francisco's Chinatown.

If you happen to be seated across from Colonel George Chow, the proprietor, his comments can make the panorama below even more intriguing.

"See the man wheeling that pushcart down the street there?" I obediently turned by head. "He's one of the richest men in Chinatown, a millionaire with a mansion out in Sea Cliff. But there he is, pushing his own cart. Chinatown is like that—full of characters."

Colonel Chow, who opened the Golden Pavilion in 1964, had a distinguished military career before entering the restaurant business. Now he concentrates his interest on his restaurants (there is another Golden Pavilion in Los Altos, south of San Francisco) and on his Chinese cooking seminars.

He emphasizes that Chinese cooking is an art and that recipes should be adapted both to the available ingredients and the inspiration of the moment. As he puts it, "It is our fervent wish that each cook will prepare each dish to his or her taste, adding or rejecting as the creative spirit dictates. It is also our hope that once the basic approach to Chinese cooking is learned, it will open the door to the entire spectrum of Chinese food."

The menu at the Golden Pavilion offers both northern and southern Chinese cuisine and features such distinctive dishes as Beef-Tomato-Curry Noodles, Golden Pavilion Prawns (which are sautéed with slivers of onion and Chinese parsley), and Yang Chow Fried Rice (which contains peas, bits of prawns, barbecued pork, and green onion). And the Golden Pavilion's Ginger Ice Cream is a dessert fit for the gods.

CHING CHOW SHRIMP

1 pound shrimp	2 tablespoons oil
½ teaspoon salt	1 inch fresh ginger root,
dash white pepper	thinly sliced
1 teaspoon cornstarch	2 tablespoons chicken broth
1 egg white	few drops sesame seed oil
1 cup peas, shelled or frozen	(optional)

Shell shrimp and devein them by making a shallow cut down the back and lifting out the black and white intestinal vein with the knife point. Wash shrimp and dry carefully. Combine salt, pepper, cornstarch, and egg white in a bowl. Add shrimp and toss them in the mixture until well coated.

Drop peas in boiling water and boil rapidly for 5 minutes. Drain. If frozen peas are used, simply defrost.

Place wok or skillet over high heat. When pan is hot, add oil. It should sizzle at once. Add ginger slices and stir-fry for 30 seconds. Remove ginger from the pan and discard. Add shrimp and stir-fry 2 minutes. Add peas and stir-fry for 1 minute.

Add the broth to remaining cornstarch mixture and stir. Add broth-cornstarch mixture to the pan. Cook rapidly, stirring, for 1-2 minutes until sauce thickens and covers shrimp with a transparent glaze. Do not overcook. Season with a few drops of sesame oil to taste. Serve immediately.

Serves 3 as the only course with rice or 6 in a full Chinese menu.

SZECHWAN PEPPER PRAWNS

2 egg whites	3 cloves garlic, minced
1 tablespoon cornstarch	10 green onions, thinly sliced
1 teaspoon plus 1 pinch salt	(including some of the
2 pounds prawns, shelled and	green tops)
deveined	1 tablespoon Szechwan Pepper
¼ cup thinly sliced fresh	Sauce*
ginger root	¼ teaspoon MSG (optional)
2 ounces vodka or bourbon	1 teaspoon sugar
3 tablespoons cooking oil	1 cup catsup

*Szechwan Pepper Sauce is available in most Chinese and some gourmet markets. If you can't find it, hot chili oil (see p. 24) may be substituted.

Mix together in a bowl the egg whites, cornstarch, and pinch of salt. Add prawns and stir to cover. Marinate for 10-15 minutes.

At the same time, marinate ginger root in vodka or bourbon for 10-15 minutes. Place wok or skillet over high heat. When pan is hot, add the oil. Add 1 teaspoon salt and heat to smoking temperature. (Discard ginger.) Add ginger marinade, garlic, green onions, and Szechwan Pepper Sauce, stirring constantly for 1-2 minutes.

Add prawns, MSG, and sugar. Stir for 1 minute or until the prawns begin turning pink. Add catsup, stirring until thoroughly blended. Serve immediately.

Serves 4 as a single course or 4-8 in a full Chinese menu.

DRY SAUTÉED PRAWNS

1 pound prawns (16-20 prawns)	½ teaspoon salt
1 clove garlic	¼ teaspoon white pepper
1 teaspoon minced fresh	2 tablespoons cooking oil
ginger root	3 green onions, cut into
2 tablespoons dry sherry	1-inch sections

Clean and devein prawns by slitting back and removing intestine, but leave shell and tail intact.

Crush or mince the garlic.

In a bowl combine the garlic, minced ginger, sherry, salt, and pepper and marinate prawns in the mixture for 15 minutes.

Place wok or skillet over high heat. When pan is quite hot add the oil. Add prawns and toss-fry until pink, about 30 seconds. Add garlic, ginger-sherry mixture, and onions. Stir until prawns are coated with a glossy brown glaze. The shells keep the prawns tender and moist, acting almost as a steamer. Serve at once.

Serves 2 as a whole meal with rice or 4-6 as part of a full Chinese menu.

HUNAN
853 Kearny Street
415-788-2234

I had an Irish grandmother who made a mean apple pie, but always preferred a brisk round of poker to a stint over a hot stove. Fortunately for those who like daring food, Henry Chung's grandmother was cut from a different cloth. Her recipes make up the repertoire of Hunan, one of San Francisco's smallest and least pretentious restaurants.

Henry and his wife, Diana, are from the province of Hunan, which is located between Szechwan and Canton in the south central section of China. Their tiny dining room was the first in California to be devoted entirely to Hunan's peppery food, the lusty flavors of which are closely allied to the combustible seasonings of Szechwan. Hunan specializes in smoked, steamed, and dry-sautéed foods whose characteristic taste comes from hot black bean sauce or the zing of a specially prepared red-hot sauce.

The menu offers smoked chicken, ham, or duck, cooked with black bean and garlic sauce. Steamed spareribs are a favorite, as is the chicken and cucumber salad. Steamed buns, slightly larger than pot stickers (see page 67), are filled with spicy meat and vegetable mixtures. If you're feeling especially bold order Hunan smoked sausages with hot sauce. After you've eaten your fill you can dampen the fire in your throat with one of the three available desserts: Hunan dumplings, fermented sweet rice, or thin onion cakes.

Hunan is a rich, abundant land and the farmers there are attached to their soil. Only in recent years have immigrants from the area begun to arrive in this country, bringing with them their distinctive cuisine. San Francisco is lucky that two of them, Henry and Diane Chung, chose to make this city their home, for the Hunan is a significant addition to its roll of restaurants.

HUNAN CUCUMBER SOUP

6 large dried mushrooms
2 cucumbers, peeled, seeded,
   cut into thin slices and
   then 1-inch squares
¾ cup very lean Virginia ham,
   cut into shreds

1½ quarts chicken broth
¾ teaspoon salt
1 tablespoon soy sauce
¼ cup green onions, chopped
few drops sesame seed oil
black pepper to taste

In a small bowl, cover mushrooms with warm water and soak for 30-45 minutes. Drain mushrooms and pat dry with paper towels. Remove the stems and cut mushrooms into quarters.

Place chicken broth in a large, heavy saucepan and add cucumbers, mushrooms, and shredded ham. Bring to a boil. Reduce heat to low, partially cover the pan, and simmer for 15-20 minutes.

Add salt to taste and soy sauce. Before transferring soup to a tureen, add chopped green onions, a few drops of sesame seed oil, and some black pepper.

Serves 6.

SHREDDED PORK WITH RED PEPPERS

½ pound lean pork, cut in
   thin diagonal slices

MARINADE
1 tablespoon soy sauce
1 tablespoon cornstarch

SAUCE
2 tablespoons soy sauce
1 tablespoon white wine
1 tablespoon apple cider
1 teaspoon cornstarch
½ teaspoon sugar
½ teaspoon salt

1½ teaspoons Chinese red
   pepper powder
1 tablespoon fermented black
   beans (soaked 10 minutes,
   rinsed, and drained)

2 or 3 red (if available) or
   green peppers, cored,
   seeded, and cut in thin
   strips

3 cups oil for frying

Cut pork in shreds and place in the marinade mixture for 15 minutes.

Blend all sauce ingredients together in a small bowl and keep handy.

Heat oil in a skillet or wok. Drain off excess marinade from the pork and fry for 25-30 seconds. Remove pork and pour off all but 2 tablespoons of the oil. Stir-fry shredded bell pepper until half done. Return pork to pan, stir quickly, and add sauce mixture. Stir over medium-high heat until sauce has thickened.

Serves 2 as a main dish or 4-6 with accompaniments on a Chinese menu.

CHICKEN AND CUCUMBER SALAD

¼ ounce dried agar-agar
1 cup peeled, seeded shredded
   cucumber

1 cup cooked shredded chicken
2 tablespoons cooked shredded
   ham

DRESSING

2 tablespoons sesame seed
   paste (this is also sold as
   "taheeni" in Middle
   Eastern markets)
2 tablespoons soy sauce

1 tablespoon Chinese mustard
   powder (or to taste)

1 tablespoon vinegar
½ teaspoon salt
1 tablespoon sesame seed oil
½ teaspoon chili oil (see p.24)
1 clove garlic, mashed

Cut agar-agar in 1-inch pieces. Soak in warm water for 15-25 minutes. Squeeze dry and lay on a plate. Arrange cucumber, chicken, and ham shreds on top. Place in the refrigerator to cool.

Mix together the dressing ingredients in a cup or bowl. Stir very thoroughly.

Pour dressing and mustard powder over salad and toss vigorously.

Serves 2 as a main course luncheon dish.

JOE JUNG'S
881 Clay Street
415-362-6706

Taking a stroll through Chinatown is a good way to galvanize your appetite. Glistening bronze ducks hang in the market windows and lively fish sparkle in the sunlight as they take their last swim in a fishmarket tank before appearing on someone's dinner plate. Tantalizing aromas waft out of nearly every doorway and still life arrangements of exotic food suggest what's in store at the dozens of restaurants that dot every street and alley. When the hunger pains finally become unbearable, your only difficulty will be deciding which restaurant to try.

Faced with that decision one night, my husband and I followed a well-fed family up Clay Street, hoping they'd lead us to a restaurant we'd not yet discovered. On the way we were momentarily sidetracked by a scene so typical of Chinatown that we thought for a minute someone must be shooting a film.

Down a narrow alley two tennis buffs were playing a fast game of singles to the accompaniment of an all-girl band tuning up on the same playground. The enthusiasm of the miniature musicians almost made up for their clinkers. Across the street, several bent old men ignored this gay cacophony as they squinted through the dusty windows of the *Young China Daily* to read the newspapers pasted there.

By the time we returned to the street we'd almost lost sight of our unpaid guides. Through the dimming light we caught a final glance of them entering a restaurant called Joe Jung's. A few minutes later, feeling absurdly like Nick and Nora Charles, we followed them through the door.

Our instincts had been right. The Chinese family who had led us here clearly enjoyed good food, for the dinner we had was excellent.

There are three Joe Jung restaurants in San Francisco (two located on Market Street) and they all prosper because of the unending personal attention of their owner. This dervish of energy begins his day cooking breakfast at one of the Market Street spots, and ends it many hours later behind the stove at the Clay Street establishment, where he prepares dinner for hundreds of guests each night.

Joe Jung loves to cook and he doesn't limit himself to a Chinese menu. American food is also available here, including what is reputed to be the best fried chicken in town. I must admit I've never tried it. I can't get past the Chinese section of the menu.

PAPER-WRAPPED CHICKEN

**1 whole chicken or 2 whole
  chicken breasts**

MARINADE
2 tablespoons soy sauce	**½ teaspoon sesame seed oil**
2 teaspoons dry sherry	**1 teaspoon sugar**
2 teaspoons oyster sauce	**½ teaspoon salt**
1 teaspoon oil	**2 teaspoons cornstarch**

**parchment, wax paper, or
  thin aluminum foil
oil for deep-frying (optional)**

Skin and bone the chicken. Cut the meat into 1-inch squares and flatten each square with the side of a cleaver or heavy knife. You should have about 40 squares.

Combine the marinade ingredients in a bowl. Mix well and add the chicken squares. Allow the chicken to marinate for 30 minutes.

Meanwhile, cut paper into 40 4-inch squares. When the chicken has finished marinating, wrap each piece in a square of paper folded in the shape of an envelope. That is, place a piece of chicken slightly below the center of each square and fold the bottom point up and over the chicken. Fold in the sides and tuck the pointed top flap in to close the packet.

Now you have your choice of cooking methods. Many people like to deep-fry paper-wrapped chicken. You can fry 4 or 5 packages at a time in a skillet or wok in oil heated to 375°. Each batch will take about 3 minutes to cook. Parchment or wax paper are preferred for deep-frying. In China, they use edible paper to wrap the chicken and the whole thing can be popped in the mouth.

Joe Jung wraps his chicken in thin aluminum foil and bakes the packages in a 350° oven for about half an hour. You may like this method best, too, as it makes the preparation of paper-wrapped chicken a very simple matter.

Serves 8-10 as part of a full Chinese menu.

JOE JUNG'S PEKING DUCK

1 4-5 pound Long Island
   duckling

SEASONINGS FOR DUCK CAVITY

1 onion, quartered	1 teaspoon sesame seed oil
1 stalk celery, cut in chunks	¼ teaspoon Chinese five spices
3 stalks Chinese parsley or	2 pieces star anise
coriander	1 teaspoon salt
½ cup honey	sesame seed oil (optional)
1 cup boiling water	

ACCOMPANIMENTS
Mandarin pancakes (see p.57)
Hoisin or plum sauce (see p. 83)
onion brushes (see p. 58)

Clean duck and remove any excess fat. Bring a large pot of water to a boil and lower the duck into it for 2 minutes. Pat dry with paper towels.

Mix together the seasonings for the cavity and place inside the duck. Sew up the opening and hang the duck to dry in a cool, drafty place for 8-10 hours. Place a pan under the duck to catch the drippings.

Mix together the honey and 1 cup boiling water. Brush the duck with the honey mixture 3 or 4 times in the final 2 hours of drying. The honey will give the duck its characteristic crisp golden glaze.

Place the duck on a rack over a pan containing a couple of inches of water. Roast in a preheated 350° oven about 1½ hours. If you like, you can baste the duck every 15 minutes or so with sesame seed oil.

Remove the duck from the oven and slice off the skin in 1½-by-2-inch pieces. Cut the meat into bite-size pieces. Arrange the skin and the meat on a platter and serve with Mandarin pancakes. Traditionally, the skin is served alone, with the duck meat saved for another meal. However, these days most restaurants serve the skin and the meat together. Each guest places some of the duck on a pancake, dips a green onion in one of the sauces and places it on top. The pancake is then carefully folded over the filling so not a morsel creeps out during the critical transfer from plate to mouth.

Serves 4 as a main course or 6 as part of a full Chinese menu.

BIRD'S NEST SOUP

Despite its reputation as an agent for preserving femininity and youthfulness, Bird's Nest Soup has never really caught on in this country. For one thing, the special bird's nests required for it are scarce and dismayingly expensive. They come from sea caves in isolated islands off the coast of Southeast Asia, and gathering them is a laborious process. Then, too, the idea of eating a bird's nest doesn't thrill most Westerners. But when it comes to food, it's always wise to keep an open mind. Remember what your mother said about trying just one little bite.

¼ **pound dried bird's nest**
 6 **cups chicken broth (combined with pork broth, if available)**

½ **breast of chicken, boned, skinned, and sliced**

MARINADE
 2 **tablespoons Chinese rice wine or dry sherry**
few drops sesame seed oil

2 **egg whites**
1 **tablespoon cornstarch**

½ **teaspoon salt**
minced green onions

Soak bird's nest overnight in cold water. Clean, removing loose feathers with tweezers.

Place chicken in the marinade mixture for 30 minutes.

Bring 1 quart water to a boil, add the bird's nest, and cook about ½ hour. Drain and rinse in cold water.

Fill a bowl with boiling water. Plunge marinated chicken pieces into water for a few seconds, just to firm the flesh.

In a large pan combine broth, bird's nest, chicken slices, and salt. Stir well, cover, and simmer over very low heat for 1 hour. Garnish with minced green onions.

Serves 6.

KUO WAH
950 Grant Avenue
415-982-3706

Two splendidly dressed hand-painted Chinese lords oversee the crowd that passes through the doors of Kuo Wah every day. These distinguished gentlemen are the original work of E. C. Chen, who, after redesigning Kuo Wah, was whisked off to Hollywood by 20th Century Fox to design film sets.

A favorite with natives and tourists alike, Kuo Wah is a large restaurant made cozy by the artful use of different dining levels and alcoves. Its extensive menu of Cantonese dishes offers both old favorites and excursions into a more rarified gastronomical atmosphere.

The paper placemats that cover the luncheon tables (linen replaces them in the evening) are literally conversation pieces. They are printed with useful Chinese phrases as well as simple directions for managing chopsticks. The placemats were designed by Shirley Lewis Harris, who suggests you casually toss a Chinese phrase or two into the conversation the next time you visit your neighborhood Chinese restaurant. It may get you the best table in the house.

Here comes the waiter . . . . *Kay toy dough la*
And the owner's lovely daughter . . . . *See tao liang*
nuey dough la
Serve yourself the fried rice . . . . *Chow fon gee bin la*
And serve the soup to me . . . . *Bay dee tong*
Do you like beef with ginger? . . . . *Nee jone yee sahng*
gang gnow yuk ma?
I love the sweet aroma! . . . . *Jun ho mee*
The last is especially useful if you indulge in Kuo Wah's *dim sum* lunch. Some of the delicious little mouthfuls (most are small enough to fit in the mouth, though in some cases it might be a bit of a squeeze) called *dim sum* have sweet fillings which do, indeed, have a lovely aroma. Here are recipes for some of the delicacies you can choose at Kuo Wah's *dim sum* lunch.

SALTY TRIANGLES

FILLING

3 teaspoons dried shrimp, soaked for 30-60 minutes in water or sherry and minced	¼ teaspoon salt
	½ teaspoon MSG (optional)
3 water chestnuts, minced	6 dried black mushrooms, soaked for 30-60 minutes in warm water, minced
¼ pound bamboo shoots, minced	
1 green onion, chopped	1 tablespoon sherry
3 tablespoons soy sauce	3 tablespoons oil for frying

DOUGH

3 cups sweet rice flour   1½ cups boiling water
1 teapoon sugar

oil for deep frying

To make filling, combine all filling ingredients. Toss-fry very quickly in oil, then refrigerate.

Next, make the dough by mixing sugar with flour and adding boiling water. This makes a soft dough. Cover dough with a damp cloth and let stand 10 minutes. Roll dough on floured board and form it into a sausage shape. Cut dough into 1½-inch lengths, then roll into balls. Flatten each ball into a thin circle. Put one teaspoon of filling in each circle, fold, and crimp edges to seal.

Heat oil for deep-frying in wok or electric skillet to 375°. Deep-fry Salty Triangles, a few at a time, until golden. Drain on paper towels and serve at once.

Makes about 3 dozen Salty Triangles.

CHICKEN ROLL

These tasty little *dim sum* morsels make marvelous hot appetizers.

DOUGH WRAPPERS

2 cups flour   2½ cups water
2 eggs

FILLING

½ pound minced chicken
(cooked or raw)
1 tablespoon dry sherry
¾ teaspoon salt
1 teaspoon cornstarch
5 tablespoons vegetable oil
½ cup finely minced leeks or
green onions

2 cups shredded bamboo shoots
1 cup shredded mushrooms
(fresh or dried—if dried, presoak in hot water)
2 cups bean sprouts
2 tablespoons soy sauce

oil for deep frying

To make the dough wrappers, beat together the flour, eggs, and water until smooth. Grease a 7-inch skillet (a crepe pan is perfect) and place over medium heat. Pour enough batter into the pan just to cover—wrapper should be *very* thin. Fry on one side only and remove from pan as soon as it sets. Place on cooling rack.

Mix together all filling ingredients and place 2 tablespoons of the filling near the center of each wrapper. Fold lower edge up and left and right edges over to form a neat packet. Seal the edges by moistening and pressing with your fingertips.

Heat oil for deep-frying in a skillet or wok over medium-high heat until a cube of bread dropped in the oil causes it to foam (375°F). Fry chicken packets four or five at a time for 3 minutes or until golden. Remove and drain on paper towels while frying the remaining Chicken Rolls, or *Gai Goon.*

Makes about 3 dozen Chicken Rolls.

KUO WAH BARBECUED SPARERIBS

2 pounds spareribs

MARINADE

2 tablespoons Hoisin sauce
½ teaspoon salt
1 clove garlic, minced or
pressed
½ teaspoon minced fresh
ginger (or ¼ teaspoon powdered Jamaican ginger)

3 tablespoons soy sauce
1 tablespoon sherry or Chinese
rice wine
3 tablespoons honey
2 tablespoons catsup

Blend together all marinade ingredients and marinate spareribs for at least 4 hours or overnight.

To barbecue in the oven in the Chinese manner, fashion S-shaped hooks of heavy wire (those ubiquitous wire coat hangers work nicely) and hang ribs in the oven from the upper rack. Place a shallow pan on the bottom of the oven to catch the drippings. Roast in a preheated 375° oven for 15 minutes, then lower temperature to 350° and continue roasting for another 30-35 minutes.

If you don't want to bother hanging the ribs, they can be spread in a single layer in a shallow pan and roasted in a 375° oven for 45 minutes-1 hour. Remember to turn them frequently.

Serves 4 as an appetizer or 2 as a main course.

THE MANDARIN
Ghirardelli Square
900 North Point
415-673-8812

When Madame Cecilia Chiang opened the first Mandarin in San Francisco in 1961, other Chinese restaurant owners wished her well but secretly shook their heads in wonder at her innocence. First, she had chosen an impossible location, far from the established ground of Chinatown; and second, she proposed serving what was then a totally unfamiliar cuisine—that of northern China. A menu offering such startling dishes as Beggar's Chicken, Sizzling Rice Soup, Hot Pepper Prawns, and Mongolian Lamb, rather than old faithfuls like Sweet and Sour Pork or *Chow Mein*, surely spelled disaster.

But Madame Chiang had correctly assessed San Franciscans as an adventurous lot. The Mandarin survived—and flourished to the point where, in 1968, it moved to its present quarters in Ghirardelli Square, the old chocolate factory that now houses a colorful assortment of exclusive shops and restaurants.

The interior of the new Mandarin provides a setting to match the refinement of its cuisine. Retaining the softly rose-hued brick walls and wooden ceiling beams of the original building, Madame Chiang went on to fill the restaurant with such treasures as wooden temple carvings and tapestries embroidered in the "Forbidden Stitch" (which is so minute that young girls who practiced it in old China eventually lost their sight).

Although the style of cooking Madame Chiang brought to San Francisco is often called *Mandarin*, it is really made up of specialties from several Chinese provinces. "The cuisine of the Mandarin classes was a combination of the cuisine of the capital, augmented by the specialties of every province: the finest produce, from the limitless resources of the whole of China, prepared by chefs whose skill had been handed down from time immemorial," writes Cecilia Chiang in her cookbook-memoir, *The Mandarin Way*.

The tradition of passing on dishes is being continued by the

Mandarin, for many of the chefs and owners of newer Chinese restaurants once worked in the Mandarin's kitchen. Since Madame Chiang introduced San Francisco to northern and western Chinese food almost fifteen years ago, smaller restaurants specializing in the unique preparations of Hunan, Szechwan, Peking, and Mongolia have followed the way, becoming welcome additions to the city's restaurant scene. Now with the establishment of a second Mandarin in Beverly Hills, Madame Chiang will probably open the door for a rash of fascinating Chinese restaurants in Los Angeles.

MANDARIN SWEET-SOUR FISH

This exquisitely delicate dish might serve as the main course at a dinner party, although in China a whole fish is most often one of the last courses at a banquet. Mandarin Sweet-Sour Fish is also a traditional part of the menu at New Year's Eve festivities.

1 rock cod, sea bass, carp,
  or red snapper, 3-3½
  pounds
1 egg (optional)

¼ cup cornstarch
¼ cup Chinese rice wine or dry
  sherry or water (optional)
oil for deep-frying

GARNISH
carrots, finely sliced
celery, finely sliced

SAUCE
¾ cup sugar
½ cup Chinese wine vinegar
  or cider vinegar
½ cup catsup
½ cup water

Juice of 1 lemon
1 teaspoon soy sauce
  (optional)
¼ cup cornstarch mixed with
¼ cup water

A 3-pound fish is the best choice for this dish. At most, the fish should not weigh more than 3½ pounds. To be sure the fish is straight from the sea, look at the eyes and make sure they are bright and clear and protrude from the head. If they are sunken and clouded, reject the fish at once. Also look at the gills and see that they look fresh and pink. Ask your fish purveyor to gut the fish and scrape off the scales, but not to remove the head and fins. Part of the attraction of this dish is that it should look as though it is still swimming.

You can, if you like, prepare the garnish first, although there is plenty of time to do it while the fish is cooking. Slice medium-size carrots and the whitest possible celery into strips as fine as toothpicks and refrigerate them, covered, until serving time.

The next stage is to lay the fish on a chopping block, holding the head firmly in a cloth since it is apt to slip, and with a Chinese cleaver or a very sharp knife make an incision about an inch below the gills. Have the blade of your cleaver or knife upright and almost parallel to the side of the fish. When the skin is penetrated, slice in a semicircular motion across the width of the fish with the blade angled slightly inward. This makes a deep slash to the bone. Repeat the slashing at 1-inch intervals—there will be 5 or 6—down the fish on both sides.

Now hold the fish up by the tail so the slashes open up like a flower and sprinkle cornstarch into the slashes and over the fish. You may, if you like, substitute a mixture of ¼ cup cornstarch, 1 egg, and the rice wine (or sherry or water) and cover the fish as described, but Madame Chiang prefers the simple cornstarch method, as it produces a more attractive, fluffier result.

The fish is now ready for deep-frying. Put sufficient oil in a wok or deep-fryer to come within 2 inches of the top and heat to 400°. When the oil is hot (test it with a bread cube or fat thermometer) put the fish into the oil and cook it for approximately 20 minutes. The time will vary according to the heat of the oil and the size of the fish. Turn it occasionally to see that the slashings keep open and that every part is cooking evenly. The fish will emerge a beautiful golden brown and can be set aside while the sauce is being prepared. Press the fish down a little so it will lie flat when it's served.

To make the sauce, combine the sugar, vinegar, catsup, water, lemon juice, and, if you wish to include it, the soy sauce, in a wok or saucepan. Don't use Japanese wine vinegar as it's too sweet and will spoil the balanced flavor of the sauce. Bring the ingredients to a boil over medium heat and simmer for a minute or less, stirring constantly, as the sugar burns easily. Stir the blended cornstarch and water into the sauce and cook until it thickens.

After covering the fish with the glistening sauce, arrange the slivers of carrot and celery in a decorative pattern along the back on either side. The contrasting colors of orange and greenish white give the fish a handsome appearance to match its superb flavor. *Serves 6 as a main course or 10-12 in a full menu.*

STIRRED EGG AND PORK WITH MANDARIN PANCAKES

PANCAKES
1½ **cups hot water**
  4 cups all-purpose flour
  2 tablespoons sesame seed oil

FILLING

2 ounces dried wood ears	**1 tablespoon Chinese rice wine**
2 ounces dried tiger lily buds	**or dry sherry**
(*golden needles*)	**4 well-beaten eggs**
2 cups chicken stock	**3 green onions, chopped**
1 generous tablespoon oil	**1 tablespoon soy sauce**
¼ **pound pork loin, slightly**	**1 or 2 drops sesame seed oil**
marbled, thinly sliced	
against the grain	

plum sauce (see p. 83)

To make the pancakes, add the water to the flour slowly and mix until the dough has a springy texture. Flour a board lightly and knead the dough with the heel of the hand for 3 or 4 minutes. Cover the dough and allow it to rest for about 10 minutes. Divide the dough in half and roll each half into a cylinder 15 or 16 inches long. Slice each cylinder into 1-inch rounds and flatten each with the heel of your hand. Brush the top of the rounds with a few drops of sesame seed oil and join them in pairs, sandwich-style, oiled sides in.

On a floured board, roll out each sandwich-pancake into a thin 7-inch circle. Preheat a well-seasoned skillet (do not grease it) over low heat and cook each sandwich-pancake for 3-4 minutes on each side. Remove from the skillet and pull the two halves of the pancake apart. (The pancakes can be made ahead of time and frozen, then reheated when required.)

Presoak the wood ears in lukewarm water for one hour (or let them stand overnight in water), and rinse to be sure no sand or grit remains. Drain.

Simmer the wood ears and tiger lily buds in the chicken stock for 5-6 minutes. Drain and chop. Meanwhile heat the oil in a wok or skillet to 375°, making sure the oil is evenly spread over the sides. Put the pork and rice wine into the wok or skillet and stir-fry for 2-3 minutes. Remove the pork and place on paper towels to drain.

Pour the eggs into the pan and stir-fry quickly. Almost immediately add the pork, green onions, soy sauce, sesame seed oil, wood ears, and tiger lily buds. Continue to stir-fry rapidly for 30-60 seconds to blend the flavors. It is almost impossible to give the exact timing for the stir-frying, as there is considerable variation from one stove to another. The eggs should be just barely set when you add the other ingredients. Take care to put the ingredients into the pan in the proper order or the wood ears will disintegrate.

Bring the filling to the table on a serving dish. Tuck the pancakes in a napkin to keep them warm and serve on a separate plate. Each guest brushes a little plum sauce on a pancake with a scallion cut into brushes in the following way: cut off root end and green top of green onions or scallions. Make a number of parallel, vertical cuts about ¾ inch deep at each end and then make a series of similar cuts at right angles to the first ones to form a grid pattern. If you soak the onion brushes for an hour in ice water after cutting they will become frilly and make the perfect tool for spreading the delicious plum sauce, which is available in cans and jars at Chinese markets. If you cannot find plum sauce in your area (or you don't want to make it) you can substitute a tart chutney. It won't be the same, but it will still be a treat.

The guests then put some of the filling on a pancake and roll it into a plump tube, with one end tucked in. It is best eaten by hand—and even then it's a challenge to keep the filling in if you've been greedy. But this *Mu-Shi* Pork is well worth any compromise of dignity it may require.

Serves 6 as an entrée or 12 as part of a Chinese menu.

BEGGAR'S CHICKEN

The name of this dish reveals its humble origins, for in earlier times when a beggar was lucky enough to obtain a chicken but had no means of cooking it, he would pack it in wet clay and bake it in a fire, thereby removing the feathers and sealing in the bird's delicious juices. No beggar would recognize the Mandarin's version, with its elegant stuffing of black mushrooms, snow peas, ham, water chestnuts, and spices, but the moment when the clay is cracked, releasing the chicken's fragrance, still is as exciting as it must have been for the rogue who first tried it with a pilfered fowl.

1 3-pound frying chicken	¼ teaspoon five spice powder
1 tablespoon yellow rice wine or sherry	1 tablespoon soy sauce
1 heaping teaspoon salt	1 pound ceramic clay (available in most art supply
1 teaspoon sesame seed oil	stores)

STUFFING

¼ cup Virginia ham (the nearest equivalent to Chinese *Chinhua* ham)	¼ cup water chestnuts
¼ cup bamboo shoots	¼ cup presoaked black mushrooms (cover with warm water and let stand 10 minutes)

Wash the chicken inside and out and pat dry with paper towels. Don't cut the skin anywhere, other than cutting off the tailpiece and trimming the tips of the wings and the neck opening. Combine the rice wine, salt, sesame seed oil, five spice powder, and soy sauce and rub the entire bird, inside and out, with the mixture, reserving any you have left to add to the stuffing.

Slice all the stuffing ingredients to the same size—about 1 inch long and not more than ¼ inch wide or thick. After stuffing the bird with this mixture, do not sew it up but re-form it into its natural shape by molding it and cradling it in your hands.

Wrap the bird in a piece of aluminum foil large enough to envelop it completely. Wrap it in the same way in a second square of foil (in China, it was encased in lotus leaves and newspaper). Now insert the chicken into a brown paper bag. Next, mix the ceramic clay into a stiff paste by adding cold water gradually, making sure it is not too watery and is thoroughly mixed. Using a spatula, apply the entire mixture smoothly and evenly over the paper bag to make a casing about ¼ inch thick.

Preheat the oven for about 10 minutes at 500°, put in the chicken and reduce the heat to 475° (the oven must be hot enough or the clay will not set hard). Bake for 1¾ hours. Turn the oven down to 300° and bake for 30 minutes longer. Remove the bird from the oven and bring it to the table on a metal dish. Strike the clay sharply with a mallet and open. The chicken meat will be so tender and juicy that it can be served with a spoon. The startling emergence of the chicken from its unpromising shell will astonish your guests and secure your reputation as an accomplished Chinese cook.

Serves 4 as a main course or 6 if one of several courses.

CHOPPED SPINACH WITH SHREDDED BEAN CURD

1 pound spinach
1 cup dry pressed bean curd
dash of soy sauce
2 or 3 drops sesame seed oil

pinch sugar
1 or 2 drops Chinese vinegar or
cider vinegar

Wash the spinach thoroughly to remove all traces of grit and cut off the ends of the stems, leaving the red veins at the base of the leaves. Cook, covered, in a few drops water for 2-3 minutes. Drain and press out water. Cool. Mince the spinach and dry pressed bean curd. Place in a bowl and toss with the soy sauce, sesame seed oil, sugar, and vinegar and serve cold.

Serves 6 as part of a Chinese menu.

NAM YUEN
740 Washington Street
415-781-5636

Not long ago I had lunch at Nam Yuen with a friend who had just completed a course in Chinese cooking. She looked over the menu for a moment or two and then beckoned to the waiter. Their consultation went on and on, punctuated by fierce-looking gestures indicating, I hoped, various slicing and dicing processes. Finally, reaching agreement on whatever it was they were discussing, he blessed us with a face-splitting smile and fairly danced off to the kitchen.

"What was that all about?" I asked in hushed tones, still not entirely convinced we wouldn't be hustled out of the place for causing a disturbance.

"There's a certain dish I want you to try that isn't on the menu. I just asked if the chef could make it for us as a special favor."

"Well?"

"He said he'd be honored."

That's the sort of place Nam Yuen is. Its genial, eager-to-please ambiance has made it a favorite with old China hands and the food never fails to live up to its part of the bargain. Every order is individually prepared with the freshest possible ingredients (the kitchen has a large tank where fresh water fish swim out their last moments, happily unaware of their impending fate).

A daily supply of dewy produce arrives at Nam Yuen directly from farms in nearby San Leandro and Hayward. As you might expect, the vegetable dishes are remarkable.

Unless you have some esoteric craving like Fran did, you'll find the standard menu sufficiently diverse and interesting. A broad selection including string beans with beef, clams in a garlic and wine sauce, chicken with Mandarin sauce, spareribs glazed with a spicy black bean sauce, and one of the most requested dishes, Mongolian Lamb, assures something for every taste.

MONGOLIAN LAMB

1 pound leg-of-lamb meat	12 green onions
3-4 cloves garlic, minced	1 tablespoon Hoisin sauce
1 tablespoon fresh ginger	1 tablespoon brown bean sauce
juice (see p. 7)	1 teaspoon soy sauce
1 tablespoon dry sherry	3 tablespoons oil

Slice lamb 1/8 inch thick and into 1-1½-inch squares. Mix together minced garlic, ginger juice, and sherry, and marinate the lamb in this combination for 1 hour.

Cut green onions into 1¼-inch pieces.

In a small bowl, mix together the Hoisin sauce, brown bean sauce, and soy sauce.

Place wok over high heat and add oil. When oil sizzles, add the meat and onions. Toss-fry for 2 minutes, then add the Hoisin, brown bean, and soy sauce mixture. Cook, tossing and folding, for 1 minute. Serve on a bed of fresh, sliced tomatoes.

Serves 2 as a single course or 4-6 in a full menu.

NORTH CHINA

2315 Van Ness
415-673-8201

531 Jackson
415-982-1708

One of my most treasured memories is of the time I was invited into the North China's kitchen to watch the owner and chef, Chung Kien Lee, conjure up an order of candied sugar apples. I perched on a stool to view an act that once could have played The Palace. Part prestidigitator, part juggler, and all smiles, Mr. Lee whisked the apples from a deep-fry bath into hot syrup before splashing them into the ice water that turned the sugar into gossamer strands.

The North China is a family operation, with mama running the original restaurant on Jackson Street while father and son David break in the new operation on Van Ness. Over the years the Jackson Street site has built a reputation for serving extremely authoritative northern and western Chinese food. The recent addition now makes that same cuisine available in a beautifully planned and spacious dining room.

A garden of greenery and beautiful wood partitions carved to resemble a forest sections off the large space into quiet, private areas. A fascinating painting called *The Emperor's Journey* covers one wall. Painted by Kuing Shih from a work by Tong Dy, it includes accurate representations of every tree that grows in China.

The menu of both restaurants is formidable. Tea Duck, Szechwan Style; Fried Sliced Fish in Sour Sauce; *Chow San Shen*, with its subtle blending of chicken, shrimp, abalone, and zucchini; Sizzling Rice Soup, Ming's Beef, and Fried and Baked Prawns are just a few of the treats the North China can provide for you. And don't forget the candied apples.

SIZZLING RICE SOUP

This flamboyant soup always causes a round of ohs and ahs when it's presented at the table, for when the hot broth is poured over the rice crusts it makes a lively, sizzling sound.

1 tablespoon oil	**¼ cup canned button mush-**
2 cups hot cooked rice	**rooms**
6 cups chicken broth	**sugar**
½ cup shredded chicken meat	**salt**
¼ cup bay shrimp (tiny frozen	**MSG (optional)**
shrimp may be substituted)	**oil for deep-frying**
¼ cup green peas	

To make rice crusts, film the bottom of a baking pan with 1 tablespoon oil and place a ½-inch layer of rice in it. Pat it down firmly. Bake in a preheated 250° oven until the rice is dry (about 2 hours). Cut into 2-inch pieces and set aside. Rice crusts are also formed when rice sticks to the bottom of the pan in which it's boiled. Reserve and refrigerate crusts each time you cook rice to use in this recipe.

In a deep pot bring the chicken broth to a boil and add the remaining ingredients, seasoning with sugar, salt, and MSG to taste. Lower heat and simmer soup for 5 minutes.

Deep-fry the rice crusts until golden. Drain and immediately place in a heated tureen. Pour hot soup over rice crusts which will sizzle explosively. Serve at once.

Serves 6.

CHINESE CABBAGE WITH SOUR SAUCE

1 pound Chinese or nappa	**2-3 tablespoons sugar**
cabbage	**3 tablespoons white vinegar**
4 cups chicken broth	**2 tablespoons white wine**
3 tablespoons oil	**1 teaspoon cornstarch blended**
½ teaspoon salt	**with 2 teaspoons water**

Use only the cabbage hearts, cut into pieces 1½ inches long.

Bring chicken broth to a boil. Place cabbage in a large pot and pour on boiling chicken broth to cover (add water, if necessary, to cover cabbage). Boil for 5 seconds and drain immediately. Heat wok or skillet and add oil. Toss-fry the cabbage for 30 seconds. Add salt, sugar, vinegar, and white wine. Stir-fry 30 seconds longer. Stir in cornstarch-water paste to thicken. Serve at once.

Serves 4 as part of a Chinese menu.

THE POT STICKER
150 Waverly Place
415-397-9985

The dish that gives this restaurant its name is a savory, filled dumpling that makes a tempting first course or snack. The name comes from the fact that the dumplings (also known as *kuo-tioh*), are cooked in a skillet that has been brushed with oil. Once the bottoms are golden brown, a splash of broth is added with a whoosh and the Pot Stickers are finished in a bath of steam. Although they look as if they would stick to the pot, these tidbits are actually quite easy to remove, and a continuous parade of them emerges from this restaurant's kitchen to fill the never-ending demand of hungry diners.

Tucked into Waverly Place, one of Chinatown's many side streets, the Pot Sticker is a simple restaurant with a warm ambiance. The kitchen crew is under the command of Ricky Tsuei, whose youthful face peers out from beneath a perfectly starched French chef's hat. Ricky spent four years as a chef at Cecilia Chiang's Mandarin; in those years he polished and perfected the skills that are now evident in the dishes that emerge from the Pot Sticker's kitchen.

After you've had your fill of Pot Stickers, you'll probably find that choosing the rest of the meal is both fascinating and frustrating. Should you have the boldly flavored Mongolian Beef or the Princess Chicken, tender pieces of chicken cubes sautéed in hot bean sauce? Would you rather sample Smoked Tea Duck or Twice Cooked Pork? The Sizzling Rice Shrimps and Mu-Shi Pork both deserve a place at your table, but how can you have them and save enough room for the Glacé Bananas? There is only one solution. Come back again with a group large enough to share all the dishes that strike your fancy. And it wouldn't hurt to fast for a week or so ahead of time.

Meanwhile, you can try these Pot Sticker favorites in your own kitchen.

POT STICKERS

FILLING

½ **pound shrimp, minced**	1 **clove garlic, minced**
½ **pound ground pork**	1 **teaspoon fresh ginger,**
½ **cup Chinese cabbage,**	**minced**
finely shredded	½ **teaspoon salt**
½ **cup water chestnuts, minced**	2 **tablespoons soy sauce**
¼ **cup green onions, minced**	1 **tablespoon cornstarch**
¼ **cup fresh mushrooms, minced**	

DOUGH
 3 **cups flour**
 ¼ **teaspoon salt**
 1 **cup hot water**

 1 **tablespoon cooking oil**
 ¾-1 **cup chicken broth**

OPTIONAL CONDIMENTS
Garlic-Soy Dipping Sauce
 (see p. 17)
Chili Oil (see p. 24)

Mix together filling ingredients. Cover and refrigerate for 30 minutes to allow flavors to blend and develop.

To prepare dough, mix together flour and salt in a bowl. Gradually add the hot water, stirring constantly. Work mixture with hands until it forms a ball. Turn out onto a floured board and knead 5 minutes. Cover and allow dough to rest for 20-30 minutes.

Divide dough into 2 portions. On a floured board, roll out the dough, one half at a time, until very thin (about 1/8-inch). Using a 3½-4-inch round cookie cutter, cut dough in circles. As you work, keep unused dough covered.

Place 2 teaspoons of filling on each dough round. Fold dough in half over the filling. Pinch about ½-inch of the opening closed. Continue to seal the curved edge, making 3 or 4 tucks as you go. Pinch edges together to make a tight closure. Set finished Pot Stickers down firmly, seam side up, on a floured board to form a flat surface on the bottoms.

To cook, place a skillet over medium-high heat and brush with cooking oil. Place Pot Stickers, seam side up, in skillet, taking care not to crowd them. Cook until bottoms are deep golden brown (about 5-10 minutes). For each 10- to 12-inch skillet of dumplings, add ¼ cup chicken broth and immediately cover pan. Reduce heat to low and steam for 10 minutes.

Carefully remove Pot Stickers from pan with spatula and serve hot, accompanied if you like by either Garlic-Soy Dipping Sauce or Chili Oil for dipping.

Makes about 4 dozen Pot Stickers.

NOTE: Pot Stickers can be frozen for up to a month. Place on a flat surface and freeze until firm then place in plastic bags and seal. When ready to serve, cook as usual but steam 5 minutes longer.

ORANGE SPARERIBS

These handsomely burnished spareribs with a haunting orange flavor are the original creation of Ricky Tsuei.

2 pounds spareribs	**2 pieces star anise**
water to cover	**½ cup chicken broth**
¼ cup soy sauce	**½ cup sugar**
2-3 slices fresh ginger	**2 tablespoons soy sauce**
2-3 green onions, cut in ½-inch	**1 teaspoon finely chopped**
pieces, including some of	**orange peel**
the green tops	**2 tablespoons oil**

Cut ribs apart, and with a cleaver chop each rib, bone and all, into 2-inch pieces (or if you're on friendly terms with your butcher, ask him to do this for you).

Place ribs in a pan, cover with cold water and add soy sauce, ginger, onions, and star anise (you can, if necessary, substitute a couple of drops of anise extract). Bring to a boil, then simmer, uncovered, 20 minutes. Drain, discarding liquid. Allow ribs to cool.

Mix together chicken broth, sugar, soy sauce, and orange peel.

Place 2 tablespoons oil in wok or skillet and heat until smoking.

Add ribs along with chicken broth-sugar mixture and stir-fry, constantly tossing and folding meat and sauce until liquid has evaporated and the sauce is thick and has glazed the meat.

Serves 2 as a main course or 4-6 as part of a Chinese meal.

HUNAN CRISPY FISH

1 2-3 pound rock cod
½ teaspoon salt

oil for deep-frying
¼ cup cornstarch

SAUCE

2 tablespoons oil
1 garlic clove, minced
3 green onions (including green tops), cut in ½-inch sections
½ cup light Chinese soy sauce

½ teaspoon ground Szechwan peppercorns or ground chili pepper
2 tablespoons rice vinegar or white vinegar
1 tablespoon dry sherry

Have fish cleaned and scaled but left whole. Wash and dry well with paper towels. Cut 3 diagonal slashes on each side of the fish, forming vents. Sprinkle inside and out with salt.

Heat oil in a wok or deep pot. Sprinkle fish with cornstarch to coat. With a Chinese strainer or wire basket, gently lower fish into oil and deep-fry for 3 minutes. Lift out and drain. Repeat frying process twice more (reheating oil each time) until fish is crisp and golden. The two preliminary fryings can be completed in advance, with the final frying completing the process just before serving. Keep fish warm while preparing the sauce.

Heat 2 tablespoons oil in wok until smoking hot. Add minced garlic and green onions. Stir-fry for 1 minute. Add soy sauce, Szechwan pepper or chili pepper, vinegar, and sherry. Cook for 2 minutes longer and then pour over cooked fish.

Serves 4-6 as a main course or 8-10 as part of a Chinese menu.

VELVET CHICKEN

When Ricky Tsuei worked as a chef at the Mandarin, he taught Danny Kaye the technique for making this ethereal chicken dish.

Now Danny Kaye is a frequent visitor to the Pot Sticker and on particularly busy nights has been known to dart into the kitchen to give Ricky a hand at the wok.

1 chicken breast	**¼ cup chicken broth**
1 egg white	**2 tablespoons dry sherry**
1 tablespoon cornstarch	**½ teaspoon salt**
3 tablespoons oil	**½ teaspoon sesame seed oil**
¼ pound snow peas	

Skin and bone chicken breast and cut meat into thin slices on the bias (as you would cut flank steak).

In a small bowl mix together egg white, cornstarch, and 1 tablespoon oil. Place chicken slices in mixture, turning to cover. Allow the chicken to marinate for 15 minutes.

If using fresh snow peas, break off tips and string them. Heat chicken broth in small saucepan until boiling. Add snow peas and cook for 1 minute. Remove snow peas with a slotted spoon, reserving broth. If using frozen snow peas , simply defrost them, dry them with a paper towel, and stir-fry them without precooking.

Heat 2 tablespoons oil in a wok or skillet. Add chicken and stir-fry until the meat is firm and has turned white. Remove chicken.

Add snow peas and stir-fry for 1 minute. Add chicken broth in which peas were cooked, sherry, and salt, keeping heat high. Cover and cook 1 minute.

Return chicken to the pan and cook until sauce is slightly thickened. Add sesame seed oil and serve at once.

Serves 2 as a main course or 4 as part of a full Chinese menu.

HOT PEPPER BEEF

½ pound flank steak	**2 tablespoons soy sauce**
2 tablespoons cornstarch	**1 tablespoon dry sherry**
3 tablespoons oil	**½ teaspoon sugar**
2 green onions, chopped	**1 tablespoon cornstarch**
½-1 teaspoon red pepper flakes	**blended with 2 tablespoons water**
½ cup chicken broth	

Cut flank steak into paper-thin diagonal slices against the grain (this is easier if the meat is partially frozen). Roll meat slices in cornstarch to coat. Shake off any excess.

Heat 1 tablespoon oil in a wok or heavy skillet. Cook flank steak slices over medium heat until just barely cooked. Remove from pan. Wipe out wok with paper towels.

Heat remaining 2 tablespoons oil in wok or skillet. Add green onion and red pepper flakes. Stir-fry 1 minute. Add chicken broth, soy sauce, sherry, and sugar. Cook for 2 minutes over medium heat.

Stir cornstarch-water mixture to blend. Return beef to pan. Add cornstarch mixture and stir over high heat until thickened. Serve immediately.

Serves 2 as main course or 4 as part of a full Chinese meal.

RYUMON
640 Washington Street
415-421-3868

Legend has it that there are certain fish who try to swim upstream in the Yangtze River. If they make it through the tortured gorge where the cliffs are high and the current particularly swift, they are magically transformed into dragons. That spot is called the Dragon Gate, or Ryumon.

Dragon Gate seems to me altogether too fierce a name for this Pekingese-style restaurant with its serene decor. The first time I visited Ryumon I very nearly slipped out of my shoes and ordered tempura, for the atmosphere is decidedly Japanese. I learned that the original Ryumon restaurant is in Tokyo, which probably explains the paper screens and natural wood in this otherwise completely Chinese restaurant.

A snug bar just off the entrance is a pleasant haven if you must wait for a table. It offers a complete stock of Asian beers and a staggering lineup of more serious stuff, ranging from Japan's Suntory whisky to Calvados from Normandy.

The diversity of Pekingese food is well represented on Ryumon's menu. Restaurants flourished in old Peking, where banquets were the official style of conducting business. Some of those restaurants made claims that would horrify today's fastidious health departments. One boasted that its stockpot had been started one or two centuries earlier, while another mere upstart could only say its stock had been in continuous use for sixty years. Happily, I found Ryumon's stock to be reassuringly fresh.

Ryumon is located conveniently across the street from Chinatown's Holiday Inn, one of the recent dubious contributions to San Francisco's skyline. You can't miss the hotel—it's the one that looks like the concrete was poured before the plans were drawn. However, I understand the beds are comfortable.

And just a few steps away you can experience some of the classic dishes of old Peking.

BEEF PEKING STYLE

1 pound beef (flank steak,
   sirloin, or filet) sliced
   ⅛-inch thick across the
   grain
2 teaspoons cornstarch
2 teaspoons water

½ teaspoon sesame seed oil
½ teaspoon sugar
¼ teaspoon salt
1 bunch green onions
3 tablespoons oil

Place beef slices in a mixture of the cornstarch, water, sesame seed oil, sugar, and salt. Allow them to marinate for 4-6 minutes.

Cut green onions into 3-inch sections, including part of the green tops, and then lengthwise into shreds.

Place wok or skillet over high heat. When very hot, add oil. Add green onions and stir-fry for 30 seconds to flavor the oil. Add sliced beef and toss-fry for 2 minutes. Serve at once.

Serves 2 with plain rice as an accompaniment or 4 as part of a complete Chinese menu.

MANDARIN-STYLE CHICKEN DICES

1 whole chicken breast, boned
   and skinned
2 tablespoons cornstarch
1 teaspoon soy sauce
½ teaspoon sugar
¼ teaspoon salt
1 teaspoon water

3 tablespoons oil
⅓ cup diced celery
⅓ cup diced bamboo shoots
⅓ cup diced green peppers
3 teaspoons plum sauce
   (see p. 83)

Cut chicken into ½-inch cubes. Make a marinade by combining cornstarch, soy sauce, sugar, salt, and water. Add diced chicken pieces and mix to cover. Allow the chicken to marinate for 2-3 minutes.

Place wok or skillet over high heat. When hot, add the oil. Add chicken and stir-fry for 30 seconds. Add vegetables and continue stir-frying for an additional 30 seconds. Blend in the plum sauce and cook, stirring for 2 minutes. (If the mixture seems too dry, you can add a bit of sherry or wine to moisten it.)

Serves 2 as a single course or 4-6 as part of a Chinese meal.

PRAWNS IN LIGHT CHILI SAUCE

2 tablespoons flour	1 teaspoon sesame seed oil
1 teaspoon salt	2 teaspoons tomato sauce
3 egg whites	2-3 dried chili peppers
18-20 medium size prawns,	oil for deep-frying
shelled and deveined	3 tablespoons oil
1-2 cloves garlic, minced	

Mix together the flour and salt. Add egg whites and mix well. Place the prawns in the batter and turn to coat completely.

In a small bowl mix together the minced garlic, sesame oil, and tomato sauce and have at-the-ready.

Cut the tops off the chili peppers and shake out the seeds (unless you have an asbestos tongue—the seeds are the hottest part of chilis).

Heat enough oil to cover prawns to 375° or until it foams around a bread cube and deep-fry coated prawns until golden. Drain on paper towels.

Place wok or skillet over high heat. When the pan is hot, add 3 tablespoons oil. Add chilis to the pan and stir-fry 1 minute or until brown. Add cooked prawns and the garlic-sesame oil-tomato sauce mixture. Stir and cook until heated through.

Serves 2 as a single course or 4 as part of a full Chinese menu.

SAM WO
813 Washington Street
415-982-0596

When all is said and done, the winner of my personal sentimental sweepstakes is Sam Wo. Surely only some blind attachment would continue to lure me back to a restaurant whose entrance is through the kitchen. A narrow metal stairway delivers you to the equally unpromising dining rooms on the second and third floors and the less-than-tender ministrations of Edsel Ford Fong, the world's most unconventional waiter.

Of course it could be the Chinese crullers that beckon me back, or the fact that for one long, poverty-stricken summer in my youth, Sam Wo's dirt-cheap prices staunchly stood between me and malnutrition. Whatever it is, I always feel better once I've eaten my bowl of *jook* and listened to Edsel yell for a while. I know I'm home.

Edsel Ford Fong is one of San Francisco's authentic characters (no other city, with the possible exception of London, treasures its eccentrics the way San Francisco does). He yells. He tells terrible jokes. He orders customers around, bullying them into ordering what *he* thinks they should have for dinner. Edsel is a Chinese Jewish mother.

Sam Wo is over 50 years old and I wonder how many other poor students have survived by eating there over the years. The name, which means "three in peace," refers to the trio of partners who started the place. For years I assumed that Sam Wo was a person and when my roommate would ask where I was having dinner that night, I'd reply loftily, "Oh, over at Sam's place."

As I mentioned earlier, the featured dish here is *jook*—that is, rice that is simmered so long that it breaks up into a thick, nourishing gruel. You can order a choice of raw beef, chicken, fish, shrimp, or cooked pork to drop into the *jook* to cook at the table. Tradition demands that you accompany your *jook* with Chinese crullers, holeless doughnuts first introduced to Chinatown at Sam Wo.

Another favorite here is the Marinated Raw Fish Salad. The truth is, the fish isn't really raw, for the marinade "cooks" the paper thin slices. It is vital, though, to use impeccably fresh fish for this recipe.

SAM WO'S MARINATED RAW FISH SALAD

When I asked Edsel for a recipe to be included in this book, he said that he only had one recipe and directed me instead to Doris Muscatine's book, *A Cook's Tour of San Francisco.* This fine book not only provided me with the recipe, for which I am most grateful, but also several evenings of enjoyable reading.

1 pound any of the following
  fish: cod, salmon, pike, or
  sea bass
¼ teaspoon cinnamon
salt
black pepper
2 tablespoons sugar
1 teaspoon sesame seed oil
¼ cup cooking oil for
  marinating
1 tablespoon pickled onions,
  diced
1 tablespoon preserved sweet
  cucumbers, diced

1 tablespoon preserved red
  ginger, diced
1 tablespoon preserved sweet
  and sour yellow ginger
  (hot), diced
1 tablespoon freshed chopped
  Chinese parsley or coriander
juice of 1 lemon
¼ pound rice stick noodles
oil for deep-frying noodles
2 tablespoons sesame seeds,
  toasted

Skin and bone the fish and cut into paper-thin slices. Mix together the cinnamon, salt, pepper, sugar, sesame seed oil, and marinating oil. Pour over the fish slices. Toss well and marinate for 10 minutes. Drain the fish and place in a single layer on a plate. Cover with diced vegetables and sprinkle with lemon juice. (Cold cooked fish may be used in place of raw fish, but Edsel would be appalled.)

Deep-fry the rice stick noodles. Add noodles and sesame seeds to the fish just before serving so they don't get soggy.

Serves 4 as a main course.

SHANG YUEN

The Cannery
2801 Leavenworth Street
415-771-4200

The Cannery is another of San Francisco's busy shopping and dining complexes. Just across the street from Fisherman's Wharf, this happy kaleidoscope of delights has something for everyone, from pâtés to piñatas. And just at the top, tucked back in a corner, is a pleasant respite from the crowds below—Shang Yuen.

Living up to its name, which means "the garden of peace and tranquility on the mountain's top," this restful retreat serves both good food and quiet ambiance in generous portions. Blessed with a naturally beautiful setting, Shang Yuen has taken advantage of it with a bank of windows that captures the views of San Francisco's fabled hills. The gold leaf walls and ceiling, rattan chairs, and bamboo blinds all help to set the stage for a meal that might once have been served in a palace in Peking.

One of the special dinners offered at Shang Yuen is Mongolian Barbecue with slices of tenderloin of beef or lamb, marinated and grilled over the Mongolian fire pit. The fire pit is a large gas grill whose intense heat cooks the meat quickly, thereby retaining all its juices and tenderness. When the meat is cooked, it is slipped into hot steamed buns and eaten by hand, rather like an oriental taco.

MONGOLIAN BARBECUE

It's not difficult to recreate the Mongolian Barbecue at home if you have a good-size hibachi or barbecue. You'll need to replace the grill with a fine wire mesh so the thin slices of meat cannot slip through. Purists would insist on using pine wood with the bark left on for fuel, but charcoal is a perfectly adequate substitute.

Each diner is given a bowl of marinade in which to dip his thin-sliced beef or lamb for a minute or two before cooking it over the grill. When the seasonings have had a chance to do their work, the meat is then tossed onto the grill and flipped back and forth with long chopsticks (or forks) until done. The paper-thin slices of meat will cook in just seconds.

¼ pound *very* thinly sliced beef or lamb per person

MARINADE

½ cup thinly sliced green onions	**1 cup water**
2 cloves garlic, minced	**1 tablespoon dry sherry**
¼ cup parsley, minced	**½ cup soy sauce**
	1 tablespoon sugar

Mix all marinade ingredients together in a bowl and then divide into smaller individual bowls for diners to use. This makes enough marinade for 4 people.

GREEN ONION LAMB

1 pound boned leg of lamb, cut into thin diagonal slices	**2 tablespoons soy sauce**
	1 teaspoon dry sherry
10 green onions, cut in 1-inch diagonal slices, including some of the green tops	**½ teaspoon sugar**
	2 tablespoons peanut or corn oil

Prepare lamb and green onions. Mix together soy sauce, sherry, and sugar in a small bowl and place near the stove.

Place wok or skillet over high heat. When pan is very hot, add the oil. Before the oil begins to smoke, add lamb slices and stir-fry for 2 minutes. Add green onions and stir-fry 1 minute longer. Pour in soy-sherry-sugar mixture and stir rapidly for 1 minute. *Serves 2 as a single course or 4-6 on a full menu.*

PEKING BEEF

1 pound beef (filet tips, flank steak, or sirloin)	1½ tablespoons soy sauce
1 small green pepper	2 tablespoons oyster sauce
1 small onion	1½ tablespoons barbecue sauce
7-8 fresh mushrooms	1 tablespoon dry sherry
1 tablespoon cornstarch	3 tablespoons peanut or corn oil
1 teaspoon sugar	

Cut beef into ½-inch cubes. Core, seed, and cut green pepper in ⅛-inch strips. Peel onion and cut in quarters. Cut mushrooms into ⅛-inch slices.

Mix together cornstarch and sugar and dredge beef in mixture. Sprinkle with soy sauce and toss beef well to coat all slices evenly.

Mix together oyster sauce, barbecue sauce, and sherry in a small bowl.

Place wok or skillet over high heat. When pan is hot, add 2 tablespoons oil. Add the beef cubes and stir-fry for 2 minutes. Remove meat to a warm dish. Add the remaining tablespoon oil and the green pepper, onion, and mushrooms. Stir-fry 2 minutes. The onion should be transparent and golden.

Return the meat to the pan. Add oyster sauce-barbecue sauce-sherry mixture. Stir well 1 minute to blend.

Serves 2-3 as a single course with rice or 4-6 as part of a complete Chinese menu.

SUN HUNG HEUNG
744 Washington Street
415-982-2319

While new Chinese restaurants are springing up like dandelions all over the city, some are old enough to have earned landmark status. A fixture in Chinatown since 1918, Sun Hung Heung is the sentimental favorite of old-timers and the pet of newcomers who think they are the first to have discovered it.

The restaurant was opened by two brothers who immigrated from Canton at the turn of the century. By the early 1900s one brother, Yun Wong, had earned his title of one of Chinatown's four Master Chefs. Today, under the direction of Yun Wong's sons Leonard and Wy Lum, Sun Hung Heung is still noted for the excellence of its kitchen and is, in fact, known as the restaurant school of Chinatown. Young men who show promise and dedication are taken into the kitchen and trained to its standards. According to Wy Lum, there are at least twelve chefs currently working in Chinatown who were trained at Sun Hung Heung, and as many as thirty have passed through during the years.

Like many Chinese restaurants, Sun Hung Heung has an upstairs room with a more tranquil atmosphere than the busy street-level dining area that caters to casual drop-in trade. The upstairs room has partitioned private nooks, each with a large round table. Although this room is by far the more elegant, it's also fun to have a late lunch downstairs where you can watch waiters take advantage of slack time by filling and folding *won ton*. Sitting at one of the back tables, behind platters piled high with filling and wrappers, their chopsticks fly back and forth filling the *won ton*. Then their fingers take over to fold each into a delicate parcel. Perhaps it's this personal touch that makes Sun Hung Heung's *won ton* among the best in San Francisco.

There's a lively bar in the downstairs area with a treasure of old photographs of Chinatown lining the walls. The sepia prints show the area as it was just after the earthquake, and while much remains the same, some things have sadly changed. Where once there was a shop across the street from Sun Hung Heung called Li Po Tai's Chinese Tea and Herb Sanitarium there is now a hot dog and fried chicken burger stand. Progress.

CANTONESE CHICKEN SALAD

This is not a salad in the American sense, but is usually served as one of an array of dishes in a Chinese dinner or banquet, where its crisp contrasts of texture provide a counterpoint to the other dishes. I also like to serve it as a cooling main course for a summer luncheon.

1 3-pound chicken	**1 bunch green onions,**
½ teaspoon salt	**chopped fine**
1 teaspoon sugar	**½ cup shelled walnuts, roasted**
2 tablespoons dry sauterne	**in a 350° oven for 15**
2 tablespoons soy sauce	**minutes**
tapioca flour or cornstarch	**½ teaspoon salt**
oil for deep frying	**½ teaspoon sugar**
½ head iceberg lettuce,	**1½ teaspoons sesame seed oil**
shredded	**½ teaspoon MSG (optional)**
½ bunch Chinese parsley	**rice stick noodles (optional)**
(coriander), chopped	

Rub chicken inside and out with a mixture of the salt, sugar, wine, and soy sauce. Place chicken on a rack and steam for 20 minutes (see p. 5). Remove chicken and cool. Coat chicken with tapioca flour or cornstarch and resteam for 5 minutes. Hang the chicken for ½ hour (or if this sounds awkward, refrigerate the chicken for the same length of time to set the flour).

Heat the oil for deep-frying in a large pan. Carefully lower the chicken into the hot oil and cook, turning occasionally, until a deep golden color and cooked through.

Cool chicken until you can handle it and remove meat from the bones. Shred the chicken meat with its crisp skin into slivers.

In a bowl, toss together the warm chicken slivers, lettuce, parsley, green onions, walnuts, salt, sugar, sesame seed oil, and MSG.

Rice noodles (*mei fun*) are available in all Chinese markets and are worth searching out. When dropped into hot oil, the thin, transparent threads expand explosively and cook almost instantly. They not only add a crunchy texture to this salad (use them as a bed for the salad and then toss them with the other ingredients at the table), but their dramatic expansion as they cook is also irresistable to children.

As Leonard Wong explained, this dish usually serves 4, although he has watched a single famished diner polish off an entire order alone. When it comes to servings, you'll have to be the judge.

CRACKED CRAB WITH CURRY AND GINGER SAUCE

1 live crab	½ teaspoon salt
2 tablespoons oil	1 teaspoon sugar
1 clove garlic, minced	3 tablespoons dry white
2 slices fresh ginger root	sauterne
2 green onions, finely chopped	⅔ cup chicken broth or water
¼ green pepper, finely	1 tablespoon cornstarch,
chopped	blended with 2 tablespoons
2 heaping teaspoons curry	water
powder	

Drop live crab in boiling water for 2 minutes. Remove immediately and plunge into cold water. Separate body and claws from the hard body shell. Remove and throw away any soft parts of the crab and discard any yellowish liquid inside the shell. With a cleaver or a heavy sharp knife, chop the crab in its shell into bite-size pieces.

Place wok over high heat and add oil. When oil is very hot, add minced garlic, ginger root, green onion, and green pepper. Stir-fry for 30 seconds. Add crab meat in its shell and stir-fry for 1 minute. Combine curry powder, salt, sugar, and sauterne and pour over crab. Stir-fry for 30 seconds. Add chicken broth and cook 5 minutes or until crab is cooked. Be sure you don't overcook the crab or it will be tough.

Stir the cornstarch and water together to blend and add to the wok or skillet. Stir until sauce is smooth and thickened.

Serves 2 as main course or 4 as part of a Chinese menu.

CHICKEN WITH PLUM SAUCE

1 3-pound chicken
3 tablespoons dry white
   sauterne
1 tablespoon catsup
3 tablespoons plum sauce*
½ teaspoon salt
½ teaspoon sugar

¼ teaspoon MSG (optional)
3 tablespoons oil
¼ cup chicken broth
1 teaspoon cornstarch blended
   with 1 tablespoon water
shrimp chips (optional)

Remove the meat from the chicken carcass and cut into 1-inch chunks. Mix together the white wine, catsup, 2 tablespoons of the plum sauce, salt, sugar, and, if you like, MSG. Marinate chicken in this mixture for 4 hours or overnight.

Heat wok or skillet over high heat. When pan is hot, coat bottom and sides with oil. Toss-fry chicken about a minute until almost cooked. Add chicken broth and the remaining tablespoon of plum sauce. Simmer 2-3 minutes. Stir the cornstarch and water mixture to blend and add to the pan. Simmer, stirring, until the sauce is thickened and transluscent.

Serves 3-4 as a main course or 6 as part of a full Chinese menu.

At Sun Hung Heung this dish is garnished with fried shrimp chips, which are available in Chinese or Japanese markets. These dried shrimp slices come in a variety of colors and are deep-fried before use. When fried, they look like a rainbow of crisp-fried clouds.

---

*Prepared plum sauce is available in most Chinese markets. If you can't find it in your area, you can make a good substitute yourself and keep it on hand. Finely chop ½ cup chutney and place in a saucepan. Add 1 cup plum jelly, 1 tablespoon sugar, 1 teaspoon vinegar, and ¼ teaspoon Tabasco sauce. Stir over medium heat until thoroughly blended and bubbly. Pour into a sterilized jar, cap tightly, and store in a cool place.

SZECHUAN
2209 Polk Street
415-474-8282

For years a pair of tall red doors on Polk Street has marked the spot where one could find outstanding Chinese cooking. This was the first location of Cecelia Chiang's Mandarin restaurant; it was from here that she went on to fame, fortune, and a restaurant in the high rent district.

"I think it must be a lucky spot," says John Lee, the present tenant, who has adorned his restaurant with a bower of live orchids and other greenery, handsome Chinese screens, and tables covered with pumpkin-colored cloths.

If the lines outside the door during the dinner rush are any sign, John and his restaurant are shoo-ins to follow in Madame Chiang's footsteps.

As might be expected, the Szechuan (like so many words translated from the Chinese, the spelling of this province is infinitely flexible—throughout the rest of the book you'll find it spelled *Szechwan*, but John Lee prefers *Szechuan*) gives priority to the cooking of this western province. And since John Lee was born in Chungking, the capital, his food speaks with authority.

The menu indicates which of the entrees are hot (most of those that hail from Szechwan are), so you can work out a balanced combination. Dishes like Hot Spicy Yellow King Fish, *O'Mei* Vegetables (named for one of the holy Buddhist mountains and the vegetarians who live there), Lantern Bean Curd, and *Ta-Chien* Chicken are proof that John Lee produces some of the purest Szechwanese cooking in town. As the menu says, "Please be assured to try any dish you desire and we guarantee you will like it after you try it!"

TA-CHIEN CHICKEN

This dish of chicken chunks with a tingling hot sauce is named for Ta-Chien Chang, considered the Picasso of the East. John Lee uses a whole boned chicken for it, though in Szechwan province they cut up the entire chicken, bones and all. I've simplified John's version a bit by using only the chicken breast, but you can use chunks of thigh meat, too, if you like.

1 whole chicken breast, boned
  and cut into 1½-inch chunks
1 whole egg, beaten
2 tablespoons cornstarch
½ teaspoon salt
pinch white pepper
1 tablespoon oil
oil for deep-frying
½ cup bamboo shoots, cut in
  1½-inch chunks
6 dried black mushrooms,
  soaked for 30 minutes-1
  hour, squeezed dry, and
  sliced
½ cup celery, cut diagonally
  in 1-inch chunks

2 tablespoons soy sauce
½ teaspoon vinegar
1 teaspoon sugar
2 tablespoons Chinese rice
  wine or dry sherry
1 teaspoon prepared chili
  paste with garlic*
  (if unavailable, substitute additional garlic and a few
  drops Tabasco sauce)
½ teaspoon minced garlic
1 green onion, minced

Marinate the chicken chunks in a mixture of the beaten egg, corn-starch, salt, pepper, and oil. Allow to stand for 45 minutes-1 hour.

In a wok or deep skillet, heat the oil and deep-fry chicken cubes until golden. Drain on paper towels. Pour off all but 2 tablespoons of the oil.

Stir-fry bamboo shoots, sliced mushrooms, and celery for about 1 minute. Add soy sauce, vinegar, sugar, wine or sherry, and chili paste, tossing and folding for several seconds.

Just before serving, return the chicken to the pan, add the minced garlic and minced scallions, and give everything a brief stir to be sure everything is heated through. The garlic and onion go in at the last minute to preserve their pungent flavor and aroma.

Serves 2-3 with rice or 6 as part of a full Chinese meal.

*John Lee recommends the version made by Lan-Chi Enterprises Co., Ltd., Taiwan. Available by mail from many of the sources listed on pages 10-11.

CHUNG KING PRAWNS

1 pound medium shrimp or prawns	4-5 teaspoons catsup
1 egg white, beaten	2 teaspoons Chinese rice wine or dry sherry
½ teaspoon salt	1 teaspoon minced garlic
1 tablespoon oil	½ teaspoon minced fresh ginger root
oil for deep-frying	
white part of 1 green onion, minced	green part of 2 green onions, cut into ½-inch pieces
12 water chestnuts, diced	1 tablespoon cornstarch blended with 1 tablespoon water
¼ teaspoon salt	
1 teaspoon prepared chili paste with garlic (see note, p. 85)	few drops sesame seed oil

Shell, devein, and score shrimp or prawns along inner edges and spread to form butterfly shapes. Marinate in a combination of egg white, salt, and 1 tablespoon oil for 1½ hours.

Heat deep-frying oil and fry shrimp until they are bright pink. Remove with a slotted spoon and drain on paper towels. Pour off all but 2 tablespoons of the oil.

Stir white part of green onions into the oil to flavor it. Add diced water chestnuts and stir-fry for a few seconds. Add salt, prepared chili paste, catsup, wine, garlic, ginger, and green onions. Stir until well blended and heated through. Add cornstarch mixture and stir until sauce has thickened. Return shrimp or prawns to the pan and stir to coat with sauce. Sprinkle with a few drops of sesame seed oil and serve immediately.

Serves 2-3 as a main dish or 6-8 as part of a full Chinese menu.

LOBSTER SZECHWAN STYLE

This treatment of lobster is described in Szechwan as having *yu-ziang*, or fish fragrance. Actually the term has nothing at all to do with fish, but refers to food cooked with lots of garlic, scallions, hot sauce, and ginger. I haven't the foggiest notion why they call the results fishy, but I trust there's a perfectly logical explanation. Some things must be accepted on faith.

1 lobster (1½-2 pounds)
1 teaspoon soy sauce
1½ teaspoons white vinegar
few drops chili oil (see
   p. 24)
½ teaspoon minced garlic
¼ teaspoon salt
2-3 teaspoons Chinese rice
   wine or dry sherry
oil for deep-frying

12 water chestnuts, cut in
   ½-inch pieces
3 tablespoons cloud ears,
   soaked for 30 minutes
15-20 frozen green peas (for
   color)
¼ cup minced green onions,
   including part of the green
   tops

With a cleaver or heavy chef's knife, chop lobster in half lengthwise and clean. Remove lobster meat and reserve shell halves, if you like, for decoration. Cut meat into 1½-inch sections. Score edges of each lobster chunk so it looks like a flower. This makes the completed dish prettier and also allows the sauce to penetrate the lobster.

In a small bowl, mix together the sauce ingredients: soy sauce, vinegar, chili oil, garlic, salt, and wine.

Heat oil in a deep skillet or wok. Add lobster chunks and water chestnuts and deep-fry for ½ minute. Reduce heat slightly and continue frying until lobster is golden. Don't overcook! Remove lobster and water chestnuts with a slotted spoon and drain on paper towels.

Pour off all but 3 tablespoons of the oil. Stir-fry cloud ears, green peas, and green onions for about 30 seconds. Add sauce ingredients and cook for another 15 seconds, stirring constantly. Return lobster and water chestnuts to the pan and heat through. Serve immediately, garnishing the platter with the lobster shell if you like.

Serves 2 as a main course or 4 with additional dishes.

DRY SAUTÉED SHREDDED BEEF

1 pound flank steak

MARINADE
2 teaspoons cornstarch   **pinch white pepper**
¼ teaspoon salt   **3 teaspoons oil**

SAUCE
2 tablespoons soy sauce   **2 teaspoons garlic, finely chopped**
1 teaspoon sugar   **1 tablespoon Chinese rice**
½ teaspoon salt   **wine or dry sherry**
1 teaspoon ginger, finely minced

oil for deep-frying   **½ carrot, cut in 2-inch slivers**
1 stalk celery, cut in 2-inch   **few drops chili oil (see p. 24)**
slivers

Cut the flank steak into very thin slices and then into narrow shreds. This is quite easy if the meat is slightly frozen.

Marinate the meat shreds in a mixture of the cornstarch, salt, pepper, and oil for 1 hour.

In a cup or bowl, mix together the soy sauce, sugar, salt, ginger, garlic, and wine.

Heat oil for deep-frying (just enough to cover the beef shreds) in a wok or skillet until almost smoking. Add meat and stir with chopsticks while cooking to keep the bits of beef separated. Cook until the shreds have turned a dark color and are dry and stiff, about 8-10 minutes. Remove meat and drain on paper towels.

Pour out all but 3 tablespoons of the oil. Add the celery and carrot and toss over high heat until the vegetables are partially cooked (about 2-3 minutes).

Add the sauce ingredients and stir well. Return meat to the wok and stir for 20-30 seconds. Stir in a few drops chili oil. Check for flavor and add more salt or chili oil if you wish.

Serves 2 as a single course with rice or 4-6 on a full Chinese menu.

YANK SING TEA ROOM
671 Broadway (near Stockton)
415-781-1111
and
53 Stevenson (between 1st & 2nd)
415-495-4510

Just around the corner from Chinatown, on the bawdy, brassy thoroughfare that divides North Beach, is the Yank Sing Tea Room. In its plain, no-nonsense atmosphere happy throngs of lunchtime customers choose from a vast selection of *dim sum* specialties.

Dim sum (spelled a variety of ways, including *deem sum, dim sun*) can be translated as "dot heart" or "heart's delight." These delectable tidbits, so perfect for lunch, tea, or as appetizers, consist of light dough or paste wrappers enclosing an astonishing assortment of fillings and are steamed or deep-fried.

When you sit down at a table at the Yank Sing you will be asked which tea you wish. If you simply order "Chinese tea" you'll miss the chance to sample one of the many varieties available here. The study of Chinese tea could take up a lifetime, but encountering teas with names like Dragon Well, Water Nymph, Eyebrows of Longevity (which is only served out-of-doors in the spring), Clear Distance, or Iron Goddess of Mercy might make it worth the time. If you like tea with a faint smoky flavor (like a good Scotch), you can order *Ponay* tea at the Yank Sing. They also serve the lighter White Chrysanthemum tea all year around, although the Chinese drink it only in the summer.

While it's helpful to know the name of a good tea to order, it's not necessary to know the names of the dishes you wish to try in a *dim sum* restaurant. Simply point out what looks most tempting to you as the trays go by. Among the things you'll be offered at the Yank Sing are *Har Gow,* shrimp wrapped in rice dough; Bean Lotus Buns; Curry Chicken Cakes; Paper Wrapped Chicken, which has an elusive whiff of orange hidden somewhere within; and Shrimp Toast. Your bill will be determined by the number of empty plates at your table when you're finished. The price for each portion is so low that you can afford to indulge in almost anything that strikes your fancy.

YANK SING EGG ROLLS

Egg Rolls were originally snacks served to family and friends as a treat during Chinese New Year.

EGG ROLL SKINS

1 egg	**½ teaspoon salt**
2 cups flour	**½ cup ice water**

FILLING

1 tablespoon oil	**6 dried black mushrooms,**
1 cup Chinese cabbage (celery	**soaked in warm water until**
cabbage or bok choy),	**soft and fleshy**
shredded	**1 teaspoon salt**
1 tablespoon water	**1 tablespoon cornstarch,**
1 pound barbecued pork (see	**dissolved in 2 tablespoons**
p. 91), shredded	**chicken broth**
3 green onions, shredded	**½ teaspoon sugar**
1 tablespoon soy sauce	

3 cups oil for deep-frying

Some creative grocers sell egg roll skins, but if they aren't available in your area you can make your own.

Beat the egg and add flour, salt, and ice water. Knead lightly until smooth and elastic. Cover dough with a damp towel and let rest in the refrigerator for 30 minutes.

Place dough on a floured surface and roll out into a paper-thin sheet. Cut into 6-inch squares. Cover with a damp towel until ready to use.

To make filling, place wok over high heat for 30 seconds, then add 1 tablespoon oil and swirl it around to cover bottom of the wok. Heat for another 30 seconds, lowering heat if oil begins to smoke. Toss in the Chinese cabbage and sprinkle lightly with 1 tablespoon of water. Cover wok and steam cabbage for 1 minute.

Remove cover and add pork, onions, and mushrooms to the wok. Stir-fry until heated through. Add soy sauce, salt, sugar, and the cornstarch-chicken broth mixture. Stir well to blend and cook until sauce has thickened. Allow filling to cool.

ASSEMBLING AND COOKING EGG ROLLS

For each Egg Roll, form about ¼ cup filling into a sausage-shaped roll with your hands. Place the filling diagonally across the center of the egg roll wrapper. Lift the point of the lower flap over the filling, tucking the point under the filling and leaving upper flap exposed. Fold in both end flaps (if you've ever done diaper duty you have a general idea of how this works) and roll up the whole package, sealing the final flap with a bit of beaten egg.

To deep-fry, place wok or deep-fryer over high heat, add 3 cups oil and heat until a haze forms on top of the oil or it reaches a temperature of 375°. Deep-fry 5 or 6 rolls at a time for 3-4 minutes, or until crisp and golden. Drain on paper towels and keep warm in a low oven while you finish frying the remaining Egg Rolls.

Makes about 1 dozen egg rolls.

NOTE: Egg rolls freeze well and are nice to have on hand to use as impromptu hors d'oeuvres. Simply cut them into smaller pieces after they have been fried; serve with toothpicks and a hot mustard or chili sauce for dipping.

BARBECUED PORK

Barbecued pork is available in Chinese meat markets, but is worth making for yourself even if you only plan to use a portion of it for Egg Rolls. The remaining pork may be thinly sliced and served with mustard sauce or hot chili sauce as a succulent and unusual appetizer.

2 pounds pork butt	2 tablespoons dry sherry
2 cloves garlic, pressed through a garlic press or finely minced	4 tablespoons soy sauce
	2 tablespoons honey
2 teaspoons sugar	½ teaspoon Chinese five spice seasoning or allspice
1 teaspoon salt	½ teaspoon red food coloring

Ask your butcher to bone the pork butt and cut it into strips 2 inches wide, 2 inches thick, and 5 inches long. These dimensions are approximate; the strips all need not be exactly the same size.

Marinate the pork in the remaining ingredients for 2 hours, turning frequently. Drain.

Preheat oven to 425°. Place pork strips on a rack over a shallow roasting pan containing some water. Roast 10 minutes. Lower heat to 325° and roast for 1 hour. Baste strips occasionally with marinade during cooking period.

Makes 2 pounds Barbecued Pork.

SHRIMP GOW

These steamed dumplings are tasty appetizers and make a fine hearty soup when floated in chicken broth.

DOUGH
  1 cup all-purpose flour
  ½ cup boiling water

Stir the boiling water into the flour and blend thoroughly with a fork (or chopsticks, if you're really getting professional).

Place the dough on a floured surface and knead for about 10 minutes or until dough is smooth and satiny. Cover with a clean cloth and allow the dough to rest for about 20 minutes.

Form the dough into a roll about 15 inches long. Cut with a very sharp knife into 1-inch sections and then cut each section in half forming 30 small pieces.

Using a well-floured rolling pin, roll each section into a 4-inch round on a floured surface. Dust lightly with cornstarch and stack. Cover with plastic wrap while you prepare the filling.

FILLING

2 cups raw shrimp, finely minced	**1 teaspoon salt**
	¼ teaspoon MSG (optional)
1 cup canned bamboo shoots, minced	**1 teaspoon sugar**
	1 teaspoon sesame seed oil
¼ cup fresh pork fat, minced	**2 tablespoons cooking oil**

Shrimp should be either minced *very* fine or put through the medium blade of your food grinder. Combine shrimp with the remaining ingredients except the cooking oil and mix well. Place a hearty teaspoon of the filling in the middle of each dough wrapper. Fold over one edge as you would a turnover to form a half-moon shape. Crimp the edges to seal in the filling. Keep the prepared dumplings covered with plastic wrap as you work to prevent them from drying out.

Cover a round cake rack with foil and brush foil with oil. Place the rack in a skillet and fill skillet with 2-3 inches of boiling water, or enough to bring the level just below the cake rack. With a sharp-tined fork poke holes in the foil to prevent the accumulation of moisture on its surface during the steaming.

Place dumplings slightly apart on the foil-covered rack (you will probably only be able to steam 8-10 at a time), cover, and steam for 15-20 minutes. The dumplings will be translucent when done. NOTE: Cooked dumplings can be frozen for up to 1 month. Place them slightly apart on a baking sheet and freeze until firm. When frozen put into plastic bags and seal. When ready to serve, thaw and steam again for 5 minutes.

BARBECUED PORK BUNS

1 cup lukewarm water	2 cups flour
1 package dry yeast	1 tablespoon sugar
1 tablespoon peanut or corn oil	pinch salt

NOTE: 1 package (about 14 oz.) hot roll mix can be used for dough.

Pour lukewarm water in a large bowl and sprinkle the yeast into the water. Stir until yeast is dissolved. Add the oil and stir into the liquid. Put flour, sugar, and salt into a sifter and slowly sift dry ingredients into the liquid, beating vigorously after each addition. When all the dry ingredients have been incorporated, beat dough for 5 minutes. Form into a ball and cover with a damp cloth. Allow dough to rise in a warm place until double in volume (about 2 hours). While dough is rising prepare the filling.

FILLING

1 pound barbecued pork (see p. 91)	¼ teaspoon MSG (optional)
	½ teaspoon sugar
1½ tablespoon soy sauce	1 tablespoon cornstarch
1 teaspoon sesame seed oil	½ cup cold water
¼ teaspoon salt	2 tablespoons oil
⅛ teaspoon pepper	

Chop pork into a fine dice. Combine soy sauce, sesame seed oil, salt, pepper, optional MSG, and sugar in a small bowl. Combine cornstarch and water in another bowl.

Place wok or skillet over high heat. When pan is hot add pork and stir-fry 1 minute. Add seasoning mixture and stir briskly for 30 seconds. Stir the cornstarch-water mixture to blend and pour into pan. Stir until sauce thickens, about 1 minute. Remove from heat and cool before wrapping in pastry dough.

ASSEMBLING

When dough has doubled in volume, place on a floured surface and knead lightly for 1 minute. Divide dough into 12-15 equal pieces. On a lightly floured surface pat or roll out dough pieces into 4-inch rounds about ¼-inch thick.

Spoon 1-2 tablespoons of filling in the center of each round. Pull edges of dough up and around filling and pinch firmly to close. Place each bun, pinched side down, on a square of foil or waxed paper. Place buns in a warm place and allow to rise for 15 minutes.

STEAMING

Place a round cake rack in a skillet. Pour in boiling water to a level just below the rack. Place a circle of foil over cake rack and puncture several holes in the foil to prevent accumulation of moisture.

Place several buns on foil-covered rack, allowing room for expansion. You will be able to steam 4-5 buns at a time. Cover skillet and steam buns for about 12-15 minutes (when buns are done the tops are smooth and glossy). Keep steamed buns warm in a very low oven while you steam the rest.

Makes 12-15 buns.

NOTE: Steamed Barbecued Pork Buns can be wrapped and frozen once they have cooled. To reheat, place frozen buns on squares of wax paper and reheat until warmed through, about 15 minutes.

YET WAH
1801, 1829, and 2140 Clement Street
415-387-8040

Like Gaul, Yet Wah is divided into three parts. The original family-style restaurant that began the story was opened by Bill Chan in 1970. When the press of hungry customers overwhelmed that location in 1973, another site two doors down the block was added. Even that annex, which brought the total seating capacity to 200, didn't provide enough space for the growing crowds and in 1975 a third Yet Wah blossomed a block further down the street. The Chans, as one San Francisco restaurant critic deliciously punned it, had built yet another wah.

The newest of this mini chain is by far the most ambitious of the three in terms of decor. Neighborhood wags, noting the vibrant purple exterior, instantly dubbed it Moby Grape. The interior bears all the trappings of a major downtown establishment (though perhaps downtown Las Vegas) complete with red plush wallpaper, black leather banquettes, and a tree growing in the center of the room.

The patrons of the new Yet Wah have that anticipatory sparkle in their eyes that signals a night on the town, while the other two more modest locations are more appealing to the families, students, and neighborhood friends who have been loyal customers for years.

The dazzling success of Bill Chan and his family is easily explained. In spite of its rapid expansion, Yet Wah is still a family affair and the standards of quality remain as high today as when the first restaurant was born. The enormous variety of Mandarin dishes offered on the menu and their reasonable prices inspire exploration and invite return visits. It's hard not to come back again and again simply to resample favorite dishes, but with such temptations as Lichee Prawns, Lamb with Shrimp Sauce, and Five Happiness Pork on the menu, even the most hidebound are likely to branch out.

The Chans arrived in the United States in 1954, after having first emigrated to Chile where the younger family members aquired Spanish names. Today sons Louis, Antonio and Arden and daughters Vida and Valencia work in the three restaurants adding an international as well as a family touch to the operations.

YET WAH SPECIAL LAMB

⅔ **pound boned shoulder**
   or leg of lamb, cut in
   ⅛ -inch diagonal slices
2 teaspoons cornstarch
2 tablespoons oil
¼ cup shredded carrots

¼ cup bamboo shoots
3 green onions, sliced
½ cup Chinese cabbage,
   shredded
½ teaspoon salt
½ teaspoon sugar

SAUCE
¼ teaspoon salt
¼ teaspoon MSG (optional)
¼ teaspoon sugar
½ teaspoon soy sauce
½ teaspoon cornstarch

2 teaspoons Hoisin sauce
1 teaspoon plum sauce
1 teaspoon tomato sauce
½ teaspoon oyster sauce

GARNISH
rice stick noodles
1 green onion, slivered

Sprinkle lamb with cornstarch and rub into the meat. Mix together all sauce ingredients and place near the stove. Place wok or skillet over high heat; when very hot add 1 tablespoon oil. Add carrots, bamboo shoots, green onions, Chinese cabbage, salt, and sugar. Stir fry for 3 minutes and remove to a plate.

Pour remaining tablespoon of oil into wok or skillet and add lamb. Stir-fry for 2 minutes, add sauce, and cook for a minute longer. Return vegetables to the wok and cook briefly to heat vegetables through.

Serve Yet Wah Special Lamb on a bed of rice stick noodles, briefly deep-fried in hot oil and removed with a slotted spoon.

Place the Yet Wah Special Lamb on the crisp noodles and garnish with slivered green onions.

Serves 2 as a main course or 4-6 as part of a complete Chinese meal.

LEMON CHICKEN YET WAH STYLE

2 whole chicken breasts,
skinned and boned
1 teaspoon oil plus 2 tablespoons oil
1 teaspoon cornstarch
½ teaspoon salt
1 teaspoon soy sauce
1 celery stalk, cut diagonally
in 1-inch sections
½ green pepper, seeded and
cut in ½-inch squares
½ red pepper, seeded and cut
in ½-inch squares

1 carrot, peeled and cut
diagonally in ¼-inch slices
2 tablespoons green peas
4 red maraschino cherries,
halved
1 teaspoon lemon juice
¼ teaspoon sugar
¼ teaspoon MSG (optional)
½ cup pineapple-orange juice
4 slices lemon
2 teaspoons cornstarch
and 1 tablespoon water

Cut chicken into 1-inch squares and mix together with 1 teaspoon oil and cornstarch. Allow chicken to marinate in this mixture while you prepare the other ingredients (or for at least 15 minutes).

Place skillet or wok over high heat. When pan is hot, add 2 tablespoons oil. Add the chicken, salt, and soy sauce and stir-fry for 1 minute. Add the vegetables, cherries, lemon juice, sugar, MSG, pineapple-orange juice, and lemon slices. Cover the pan and cook over medium heat for 2 minutes.

Blend cornstarch and water to form a paste and stir in to thicken the sauce.

Serves 4 as a main course or 6-8 on a full Chinese menu.